The Art of Woodturning

Today there is an ever growing demand for unusual hors d'oeuvre dishes. This turned tray is simple and yet very attractive.

The Art of
WOODTURNING

Completely Revised

By **WILLIAM W. KLENKE** • Instructor, Central Commercial and Technical High School, Newark, New Jersey. Author of **KLENKE'S FURNITURE BOOK, CANDLEMAKING, FURNITURE JOINERY,** and the "**Things to Make and How to Make Them**" Series.

Chas. A. Bennett Co., Inc. • PUBLISHERS

PEORIA, ILLINOIS

PREFACE

Tʜɪs is both a book of instructions and a book of projects in the art of wood turning. It is primarily intended for the homecraftsman and boys in school shops who are interested in making fine furniture and objects of beauty and utility. Architects, builders, and prospective home owners, too, will find much within these pages to hold their interest. In short, it is applied wood turning in its fullest sense.

For over thirty years, the two books on this subject that preceded this one enjoyed wide popularity. All the good material from these two books has been retained, and to this, a large number of new projects and items of interest to the wood turner and craftsman have been added, practically making this a new book.

Too much emphasis cannot be placed upon the value and importance of turned parts in connection with fine furniture; but aside from this, there is an ever growing demand for turned objects of beauty and utility, such as candlesticks, bowls of all kinds, trays, novelties, etc. Many craftsmen earn a good living catering to this business.

Simple definite instructions are given, covering all types of turning. Great emphasis has been placed on the beauty of all projects and, at the same time, each article is useful and practical. The furniture projects here shown have been chosen because they can be made almost entirely on a lathe.

I wish to express my sincere and deep appreciation and gratitude to the following manufacturers of tools and wood working machinery for the splendid co-operation given me by furnishing many of the photographs of machine operations which I consider a valuable addition to this book. They should prove of great assistance to the craftsman.

Boice-Crane Company, Toledo, Ohio

Delta Manufacturing Division, Rockwell Manufacturing Company, Milwaukee, Wisconsin

Johns Manufacturing Company, Dunellen, New Jersey

Stanley Tools, New Britain, Connecticut

Whitman and Barnes, Plymouth, Michigan

I want, too, to express thanks to my wife, Edith Elizabeth, for her assistance in helping me compile this text.

CONTENTS

THE ART OF WOOD TURNING

Wood turning is a very ancient, useful, and fascinating art, possibly the first to employ power to help shape wood into some definite pattern or design. The first lathe of which we have any knowledge was made to revolve by using a cord and bow operated by hand; then foot power was introduced, and finally our modern electric driven portable lathe was developed.

I can well remember, when I was a boy of about fourteen years of age, trying my hand at wood turning on the foot power lathe in the home workshop belonging to the father of my chum. What a thrill I experienced to see the chips fly and finally turn out a little "what-not." It was quite a stunt to push the pedal with one foot, steady yourself on the other and, at the same time, do a clean job of turning. I envy the boy of today who has at his disposal the fine portable electric driven lathe, as well as the many other portable wood working machines I knew nothing of when I was a beginner.

The art of wood turning—and it is an art—is most fascinating, but, unlike the operation of other wood working machines, it requires quite some skill in order to do good work on a lathe, since the cut is *not* a mechanical operation, but depends upon the ability of the operator to control his tool. To help the beginner acquire this necessary skill, a few simple turning exercises are given, then face plate work, rechucking, etc., so that he will soon feel at ease at the lathe and will find a great opportunity for artistic expression which should result in creating objects of unusual beauty and utility.

9

I dedicate this book to the pioneers of portable motorized woodworking machinery for the great pleasure and occupational opportunity they have brought untold thousands of craftsmen.

Chapter One

SELECTING A LATHE

THERE are a number of fine lathes on the market today, suitable for all needs of the homecraftsman. The ideal wood turning lathe (or speed lathe as it is often called) should be sturdily constructed with a heavy cast iron bed, cast iron legs;

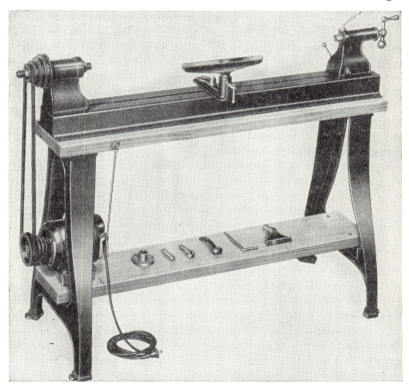

FIGURE 1. This lathe can be used as shown or without the legs and set on a bench or table.

have a heavy maple built-up top to support the bed; and shelf below to which the countershafting is fastened. It should have a stepped cone pulley and V belting, and ½ H.P. motor with switch. The distance between centers should be not less than 36″ and have a swing of not less than 12″ in the clear. Fig. 1.

It will be wise to make or purchase a pedestal tool rest for large outside turning, Fig. 2; and if you intend doing extra long work, such as tall posts, etc., purchase an extra pair of legs and an extra length of the lathe bed. Fasten these together to take your long stock. You will find it necessary to make your own built-up maple pieces for the shelf and top. Although the

FIGURE 2. Lathe equipped with a countershaft having sixteen speeds from 340 rpm to 3400 rpm for both metal and wood turning. This pedestal tool rest is ideal for doing large faceplate work. A 10-inch faceplate is now in place. The switch for operating the machine is conveniently located under the wooden top piece.

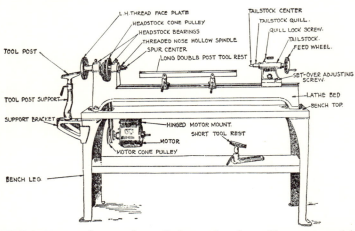

FIGURE 3. Names of parts of a well designed and sturdily constructed lathe.

·WOOD·TOP·FOR·THE·WOOD·TURNING·LATHE·

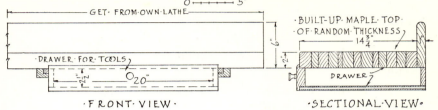

0 ⊢————⊣ 5"

·GET·FROM·OWN·LATHE·

·BUILT·UP·MAPLE·TOP·
·OF·RANDOM·THICKNESS·
14¾"

DRAWER·FOR·TOOLS

6"

2"

2½"
20"

DRAWER

·FRONT·VIEW·   ·SECTIONAL·VIEW·

| 340 R.P.M. | 475 R.P.M. | 525 R.P.M. | 675 R.P.M. |

#932
#718
#932   #720
MOTOR

| 750 R.P.M. | 825 R.P.M. | 900 R.P.M. | 1050 R.P.M. |

| 1125 R.P.M | 1225 R.P.M. | 1400 R.P.M. | 1575 R.P.M. |

| 1700 R.P.M. | 2200 R.P.M. | 2500 R.P.M. | 3400 R.P.M. |

·DIAGRAM·SHOWING·16·DIFFERENT·SPEEDS·

FIGURES 4–5

13

manufacturer will no doubt furnish a piece of soft pine or fir for these, it will pay you to make maple pieces for a more rigid job. Fig. 4.

The feed wire to your lathe should be equipped with a polarized plug (three prongs) so that the line is grounded for safety. Fig. 1.

By having a counter-shaft arrangement, you can obtain speeds ranging from 340 rpm to 3400 rpm, so that quite some metal turning is also possible. Fig. 5. As you become interested and progress in your work, you will want to purchase a compound and universal chuck. Fig. 72.

Good light is essential while working at the lathe, so, besides placing your machine near a window, it is wise to have an electric light just above the headstock, one that is fitted to a bracket that can swing around.

Chapter Two

TOOLS AND EQUIPMENT

THE tools and equipment needed for doing good wood turning should be of the best quality obtainable, since the cutting tools are often put to a great strain and, unless the steel is good and properly tempered, will not hold a keen edge.

The following list of tools, chucks, etc., is sufficient for doing any job of wood turning that will confront the home-craftsman. List given below is mostly from Fig. 6.

1" gouge
½" gouge
1" skew chisel
½" skew chisel
⅜" skew chisel
¼" skew chisel
½" parting tool
⅛" socket mortising chisel
   (regular joiners tool)
1" flat scraper
½" flat scraper
¼" flat scraper
½" right-hand skew scraper
¼" right-hand skew scraper
½" left-hand skew scraper
¼" left-hand skew scraper
½" round-nose scraper
¼" round-nose scraper
½" diamond-point scraper
6" outside calipers

12" outside calipers
6" inside calipers
6" dividers
12" dividers
Combination India oilstone
India oilstone slip
Copper oil can
10" blade, screw driver
2¾" blade scratch awl
Two foot, four fold rule
⅛" drill
1 set of power auger bits
Jacobs chuck
Compound (for metal work)
Hand drill
Grinding wheel
6" faceplate
4" screw chuck
Bell chuck
Turner's sizer

15

· W O O D · T U R N E R'S · T O O L S ·

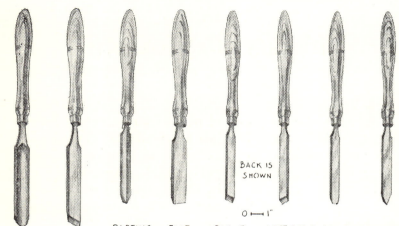

BACK IS
SHOWN

0 ⊢—⊣ 1"

·GOUGE· ·SKEW·CHISEL· ·PARTING· ·FLAT· ·RIGHT· ·LEFT·SKEW· ·ROUND-NOSE· DIAMOND-POINT·
·TOOL· ·SCRAPER· SKEW·SCRAPER· ·SCRAPER· ·SCRAPER· ·SCRAPER·

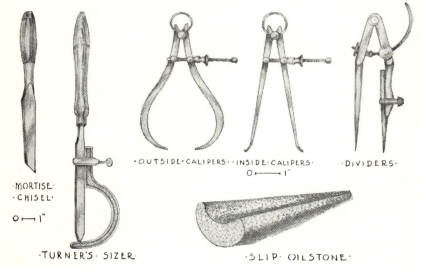

·OUTSIDE·CALIPERS· ·INSIDE·CALIPERS· ·DIVIDERS·

0 ⊢—⊣ 1"

·MORTISE·
·CHISEL·

0 ⊢—⊣ 1"

·TURNER'S·SIZER· ·SLIP·OILSTONE·

FIGURE 6

16

Chapter Three

GRINDING AND SHARPENING

Generally speaking, turning tools can be divided into three groups, (1) the roughing tools (the gouge), (2) the smoothing or cleaning-up tools (the skew chisel), and (3) the scraping tools (the flat, skew, round nose, diamond point, and other specially shaped tools used for scraping).

The grinding of all the above named tools is about the same, only differing in a few details. In every case the grindstone should revolve towards the operator, Fig. 7. The tool to be ground is held low at the start, and gradually raised to a position so that the bevel will lie flat on the stone. This angle is then maintained throughout the grinding operation. In the case of the gouge, since this tool is convex on the outside (and the bevel is on the outside), it will be necessary to roll the tool, and, at the same time, work it from one side of the stone to the other. The rolling motion makes it possible to grind all parts, and working it from side to side prevents the wearing of a hollow in the grinding wheel.

To whet a gouge, the oilstone slip, Fig. 8, is used. Hold the slip in the right hand and the gouge in the left hand.

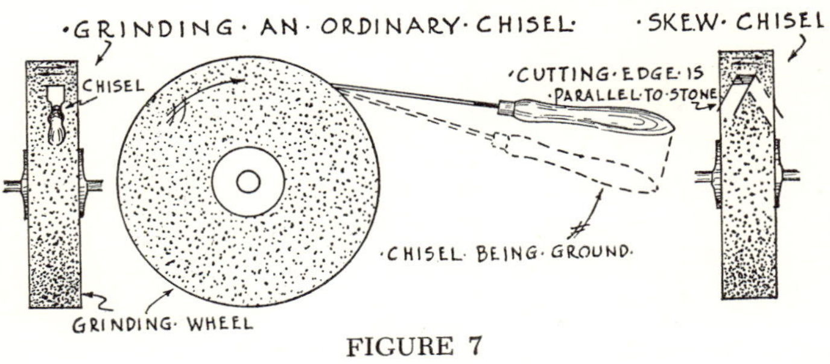

·GRINDING· AN· ORDINARY· CHISEL·   ·SKEW· CHISEL·

CHISEL

·CUTTING· EDGE· IS· ·PARALLEL· TO· STONE·

·CHISEL· BEING· GROUND·

GRINDING· WHEEL

FIGURE 7

17

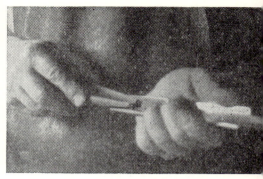

FIGURE 8. The whetstone is worked up and down while whetting a gouge and at the same time the gouge should be rotated. FIGURE 9. Remove the burr on the inside of the gouge by a few strokes of the whetstone.

·WHETTING· A · CHISEL·

FIGURE 10

FIGURE 11. The cutting edge of the skew chisel must at all times be kept parallel with the end of the stone, and the bevel kept flat.

Two movements are necessary—one to work the stone up and down, the other to roll the gouge from side to side. After some rubbing, a burr will be seen to form. To remove this burr, reverse the slip-stone and rub up and down a few strokes on the concave or inside of the gouge, Fig. 9. Repeat the entire

18

whetting operation until the gouge has been properly sharpened to a keen cutting edge.

The grinding of the skew chisel is somewhat different from that of other tools, since it has a bevel on both sides, and, as its name implies, the cutting edge is *not* at right angles to the sides. Fig. 7 illustrates the correct position of the skew chisel while it is being ground; i.e., the cutting edge is kept parallel with the top of the stone. In whetting the skew chisel, the same principle is carried out, Figs. 10 and 11.

All scraping tools are ground on only one side. The foregoing instructions hold good for the grinding, but not for the whetting. Since the function of a scraper is to scrape and not to cut, it will be necessary to let the burr remain on the tool. This burr works much the same as the burr on a cabinet or floor scraper. If the tool is properly sharpened with this burr, it is possible to work the wood down clean and quickly, especially on hardwoods, and actually cut a light shaving instead of sawdust.

Chapter Four

SPINDLE TURNING

How to Start

In order to get the most out of the stock being used, and also to lessen vibration (thereby making it easier to do the turning), it is essential to learn how to locate the center of the stock.

When the wood to be turned is square, it is a simple matter to locate the center by a number of popular methods. Possibly the one most used, especially when but one piece is to be turned, is simply to draw the diagonal lines on both ends, Figs. 12 and 13. To do this, hold the wood against the bed of the lathe or tee-rest, Fig. 14, and draw the lines with a soft pencil; or, if you prefer, use an ordinary rule or other straightedge. Care must be exercised to strike all corners at the exact point of intersection; otherwise the center of the stock will *not* be

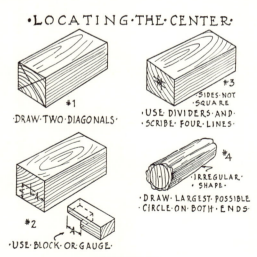

·LOCATING·THE·CENTER·

·DRAW·TWO·DIAGONALS·

·USE·DIVIDERS·AND·
·SCRIBE·FOUR·LINES·
·SIDES·NOT·SQUARE·

·USE·BLOCK·OR·GAUGE·

·IRREGULAR·SHAPE·
·DRAW·LARGEST·POSSIBLE·
·CIRCLE·ON·BOTH·ENDS·

FIGURE 12

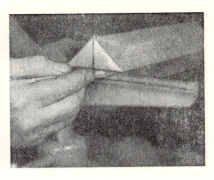

FIGURE 13. Use a rule and pencil for drawing the diagonal lines locating the center.

FIGURE 14. Tee-rest used as a straightedge for drawing the diagonal lines.

obtained. We know from geometry that the diagonals of a square bisect each other at the center.

When a number of pieces having the same size square stock are to be turned, the center can be located more quickly by gaging two lines from adjacent sides of the wood, using a marking gage, Fig. 15; or, when a great many pieces of the same size are to be turned, it will pay to make a small block as shown in Figs. 12 and 16; then, as above, draw lines with a pencil from two adjacent sides of the stock.

Often irregular shaped stock must be used; if this is in the form of an irregular rectangle, set the dividers to a distance a little less or greater than half the thickness of the wood. When doing this, place the stock on some flat surface and scribe four lines as shown, Figs. 12 and 17; then draw the diagonals of this small rectangle—or you may use hermaphrodite dividers. Fre-

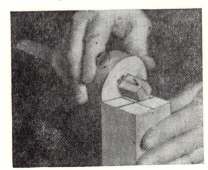

FIGURE 15. The marking gage is good to use for locating the center of many pieces of the same size.

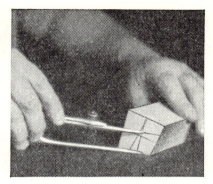

FIGURE 16. For mass production, it will expedite matters if you first make a small block as shown and draw lines from opposite sides of the stock, to locate the center. FIGURE 17. Scribe four lines as shown, with dividers, when locating the center of irregular shaped stock.

quently very irregular shaped stock, such as a branch of a tree, is to be turned; to locate the center of stock of this kind, simply draw the largest possible circle at both ends with a compass, Fig. 12.

To locate a lost center or to find the center of round stock, use one of the methods shown, Figs. 18 and 19. The center square method is the quickest. In the absence of this tool, resort to one of the other two methods. From geometry we learn that the bisector of the angle formed by two tangents from an external point passes through the center of the circle. This is in reference to the center square. Method 2 is to scribe four arcs as shown, and then draw the diagonals. In method 3, we know that the perpendicular bisector of a cord passes through the center of the circle.

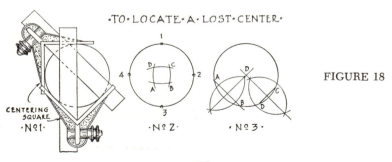

·TO·LOCATE·A·LOST·CENTER·

CENTERING SQUARE
·N⁰1·

·N⁰2·

·N⁰3·

FIGURE 18

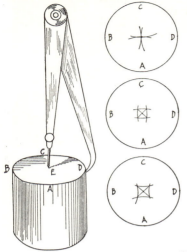

·SET·HERMAPHRODITES· SO· THAT· POINTED·
·LEG·COMES·NEAR·THE· CENTER· OF· THE·
CIRCLE··PLACED·AT· A-B-C-&D· SCRIBE·
FOUR·ARCS· AS· SHOWN· ABOVE · · · ··

FIGURE 19

FIGURE 20. In order to be certain of locating the exact center, punch a small hole at the intersection as shown, with a scratchawl and mallet.

The center having been located, punch a small hole at that point with a scratch awl and mallet. Fig. 20. Next, the wood is placed in the lathe as follows: With the aid of the ramrod, Fig. 21, drive out the live center (sometimes called spur or butterfly center); now drive this center into one end of the wood, Fig. 22 (the end where the most turning is to be done—the heavy end). File an "X" on one of the blades of the live center, and, with a pencil, put an X on the wood directly op-

FIGURE 21. Ram rod used to drive out the live center.

23

FIGURE 22. Always use a mallet when driving the live center into the wood to be turned. FIGURE 23. When turning hardwood, it is necessary to bore a small hole at both ends of the stock, to receive the pins of the centers.

posite the mark on the center. The purpose of this is to be able to take the wood out of the machine and place it back again without losing the exact center.

When hardwood is to be turned, it will be necessary to drill a small hole, about the diameter of the pin of the centers, at both ends of the stock, to prevent splitting when forcing the centers into the wood, Fig. 23. It is also a good idea to make shallow saw cuts along the diagonal lines of the live center end to give the blades of the center a better grip on the wood.

Place the live center and wood in the lathe, holding the latter with the left hand; with the right hand, turn the spindle feed handle of the tailstock out about 1″; then move the tail-stock up to the work so that the dead center (sometimes called cup center) just comes in contact with the wood. Now clamp the tailstock firmly to the lathe bed. Next, the dead center is forced into the wood by turning the spindle feed handle, Fig. 24. At this point, a drop or two of oil put on the dead center where it comes in contact with the wood, Fig. 25, will ease the friction caused by the revolutions of the wood against the dead

FIGURE 24. The wood is held in place with the left hand while being forced into the live center by turning the handle of the end spindle.

FIGURE 25. A drop or two of oil on the dead center end will prevent friction and possibly burning a hole in the wood.

center, which, of course, remains stationary. Now fasten the tailstock spindle clamp securely to prevent it from working back while the piece of wood revolves, Fig. 26.

Turn the wood by hand, so that one of the end diagonals will be horizontal; then move the tee-rest (also called tool rest), to about ⅛″ of touching the wood, having the top on line with the edge of the wood, or about ⅛″ above, Fig. 27. Clamp the tee-rest securely in place.

FIGURE 26. After the wood has been properly put between centers, tighten the quill adjustment to prevent the dead center from working back.

25

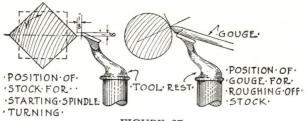

·POSITION·OF· ·STOCK·FOR·· ·STARTING·SPINDLE· ·TURNING·

·TOOL·REST·

·GOUGE·

·POSITION·OF· ·GOUGE·FOR· ·ROUGHING·OFF· ·STOCK·

FIGURE 27

Before starting to turn, try the various adjustments to make certain that all are secure; then revolve the wood by hand to be sure that it clears the tee-rest.

Small dimension stock is put in the lathe with square corners, but stock over 2½″ in size is usually cut to an approximate octagonal shape so as to lessen vibration and make it possible to start turning at a higher speed, Fig. 28. For small stock, a speed of 1800 rpm is good, provided the wood is not too thin nor too long. As the size of the stock is increased in section, length, and weight of wood, reduce the speed to start with. A few trials will soon show you what speed to use; play safe by using a slower speed. Of course, when you have had some experience, you can work with higher speeds and thereby do cleaner, smoother work.

Roughing with a Gouge

Fig. 29 illustrates a good position at the lathe. If you are right handed, carry the weight of the body on the left foot; place the right foot one short step forward. (A left-handed person reverses this procedure.) In this position, the operator has freedom of motion to rock back and forth, thus obtaining the flexibility necessary at the lathe.

Regardless of how carefully you have tried to locate the exact centers of your stock, it is always advisable to bring the

·TURNING·HEAVY·STOCK·

FIGURE 28

·CUT·OFF·THE·CORNERS·ON· ·A·CIRCULAR·SAW·TO·REDUCE· ·VIBRATION·ON·THE·LATHE·

point of a skew chisel (standing on edge), in contact with the wood as it revolves, thereby making just a slight cut on the corners. If the cut does not appear on all corners, loosen the spindle feed adjustment of the tailstock just a trifle and tap the high side lightly with a mallet. Be sure to fasten the spindle clamp securely again.

Your left hand should slide along the tee-rest, gripping the tool as illustrated in Fig. 29. The right hand is held near the end of the handle and is kept almost against the hipbone. Do the cutting out toward the ends, *not* from the ends in, for, if you hit a corner, it is likely to split the

FIGURE 29. When roughing off square stock, the left hand slides along the tool rest, tilting the gouge so as to throw the chips away from you. The right hand is held low and almost against the hipbone.

piece the entire length. Start to turn about 3″ from the end; then for the second cut come back about 6″. Do this in both directions, working from the center out.

The gouge, you will notice, Fig. 29, is tilted slightly so as to throw the shavings and chips away from the face of the operator. In order to cut a shaving, care must be taken to hold

FIGURE 30. Using the parting tool and calipers at one time. The calipers must *not* be forced, but rather allowed to slide into the groove cut by the parting tool.

the handle of the gouge low enough to actually cut rather than to scrape as would be the case if the tool were held in a horizontal position. Let me strongly advise, at this point, that the gouge be ground and whet with a flat bevel and always kept that way; otherwise it is impossible to make a good clean cut.

The Parting Tool and Calipers

In order that the wood turner may have some quick and efficient method for obtaining a desired diameter, he resorts to the use of a parting tool and a pair of calipers, Fig. 6. Where, however, a great number of pieces with the same diameter are to be turned, he often uses a combination of these tools, known as a turner's sizer, Fig. 6. If he has a sufficiently large number of articles to turn, each with several different diameters, it would be folly for him to set three or four turner's sizers, as this necessitates handling too many tools and again there would be difficulty in keeping track of the diameter of each.

FIGURE 31. After the stock has been turned to a smooth cylinder, obtain the location of the various parts by bringing the length gage in contact with the revolving cylinders as shown.

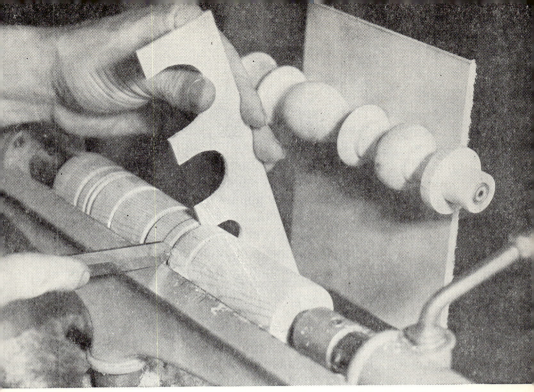

FIGURE 32. When turning to the different diameters, use the gage as shown. This gage takes the place of several different calipers and also saves time.

Where such a problem confronts the turner, he works out accurate gages, Figs. 31 and 32, with the diameters placed in the order he intends using them.

Fig. 30 illustrates the correct method for using the calipers and parting tool. Both are worked at one time, the calipers being held at right angles to the axis and resting *gently* in the groove cut by the parting tool, which is held high on the work and gradually lowered toward the center as the cut is being made. Do not press on the calipers but rather allow them to fall into place. When the diameter, at which the calipers are set, has been cut, the calipers will drop or slide through.

In order that the calipers may work freely, it is advisable to round the ends with a file; otherwise there is danger of their catching in the fibers of the wood, and being thrown some distance.

To use the turner's sizer, it will first be necessary to have the work reasonably near the desired diameter; otherwise the tool cannot be used. The use of this tool is similar to that of a parting tool in its cutting stroke, only it will be necessary to pull slightly on the handle so as to keep the caliper ends in perfect contact with the cylinder.

The special gage is used much the same as the calipers.

To set the calipers quickly and accurately, it is a good plan to use a cylinder of known diameter and set the calipers to fit over this as indicated, Fig. 33. As a matter of fact, this is the only way to set the calipers when turning to an exact diameter, as is the case when dowel ends are on a project. If you intend doing a great deal of turning, it will pay to make up a set of metal plugs that have been turned or ground to .001 of an inch of the exact measurement, Fig. 34.

The Skew Chisel, Used for Smoothing Cylinders

Up to this stage of the turning, everything has no doubt gone well for the beginner. Now for a little trouble: To correctly use the skew chisel for smoothing up stock, study Figs. 35 and 36, which clearly give the position of the skew chisel for making the cut to avoid "catching a crab" (splitting out a piece of wood). Place the skew chisel high on the wood and then

FIGURE 33. For a rapid accurate method of setting calipers, use a metal mandrel.

FIGURE 34. These metal plugs, ranging in diameter from ¼" to 2", graduated every ¹⁄₁₆", are indispensable to any wood turner.

draw it downward, gradually lifting on the handle until the bevel clears the wood, allowing the tool to cut. Always keep the toe of the chisel above the wood, thus cutting with the

31

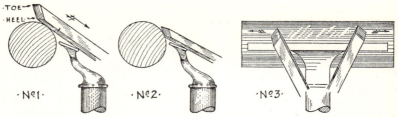

·TOE·
·HEEL·

·Nº1·

·Nº2·

·Nº3·

·PLACE·THE·SKEW·CHISEL·
·HIGH·TO·START·THEN·
·SLIDE·DOWN·TO·Nº2·

·KEEP·THE·TOE·OF·
·THE·CHISEL·FREE·
·CUT·WITH·LOWER·END·

·WORK·OUTWARD·IN·BOTH·
·DIRECTIONS· ·FIRST·CUT·
·ABOUT·4"·FROM·END·OF·STOCK·

FIGURE 35

center and lower portion of the cutting edge. Many turners work entirely with the toe forward, keeping the heel clear, but the author prefers working with the toe free.

The height at which the handle of the skew chisel is held must be governed by the bevel, whether the wood is soft or hard and if a fine or coarse cut is to be made. If held too high, the cut will be in ridges, and, on the other hand, if held too low, the tool will not cut at all.

FIGURE 36. The correct position of the large skew chisel when smoothing a cylinder.

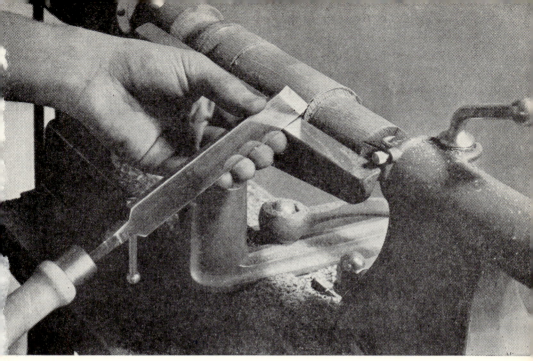

FIGURE 37. When cutting a shoulder, first make the vertical cut
with the point of the skew chisel as shown.

When cutting shoulders, first use the parting tool to obtain
the desired diameter; rough off the wood with a small gouge;
make the vertical cut with the toe, Figs. 37 and 38; then clean
out the shoulder with the heel, Fig. 39.

With all spindle turning, always (1) turn to the large
diameter, (2) cut to length, naturally not all the way through,
and (3) lay out the job with a sharp soft pencil and rule.

To avoid ruining good material, beginners should practice
using all the different tools, learn to roll a bead, and cut a clean
cove. Study the illustrations carefully, but, above all, remem-

·SKEW·CHISEL· FOR· CUTTING·A· SHOULDER·

FIGURE 38

33

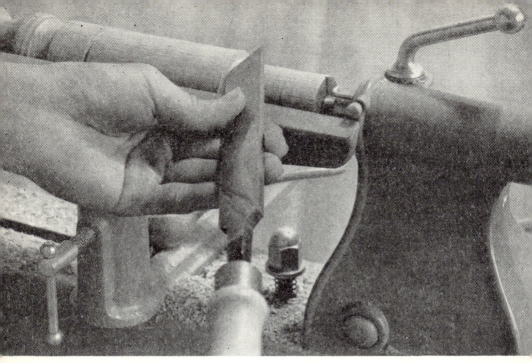

FIGURE 39. The heel of the skew chisel is used to clean out
the corner of the shoulder.

ber it requires much practice with good sharp tools in order to
do satisfactory work.

It is never advisable to cut the work free while it is in the
lathe, as the waste wood often breaks in the wrong place,
taking more wood with it than desired. It is therefore best to
cut to about $5/16''$ in diameter; then remove the work from the
lathe and do the final cutting off with a saw and sloyd knife.

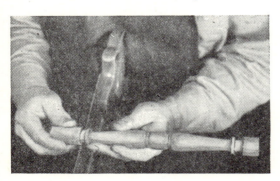

FIGURE 40. A good
way to cut off the waste
stock. Hold the back-
saw against the bench
with your body; then
work the turned piece
back and forth.

34

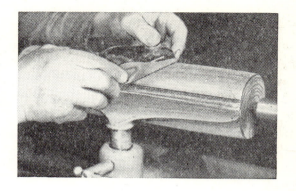

FIGURE 41. Sometimes it will help to use a block plane to obtain a smooth cut on a gnarly piece of wood.

Fig. 40. Even at this point, great care must be taken to use a sharp knife and cut cautiously.

It must be remembered, since the driving power is at the live center, this end should be weakened last and never cut to quite as small a diameter as the dead center end, Fig. 41.

The Skew Chisel for Cutting V's and Beads

Having indicated with a pencil line the location and width

FIGURE 42. Cutting a V. The ½" skew chisel is used. First the tool rests on its edge and the point makes a cut in the center; then, with a slicing motion, cuts are made on both sides.

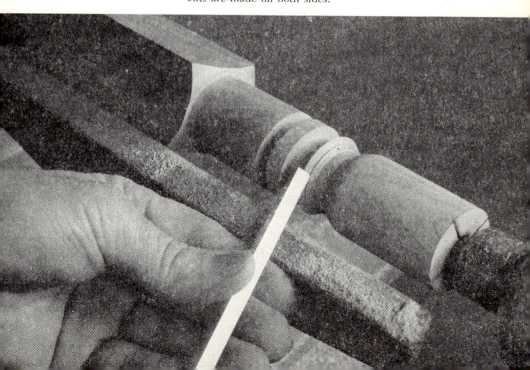

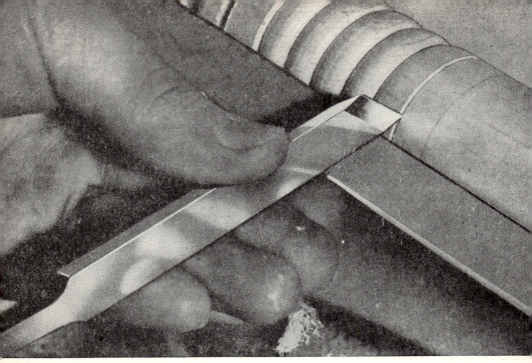

FIGURE 43. Steps taken when rolling a bead, as it is commonly called. The point of the skew chisel makes the cut at both sides of the bead.

of the V (see Plate 1), hold the ½" skew chisel on its edge and, using the point of the tool, make a cut, which will be the center of the V. Now, using the heel of the chisel and holding the tool at the proper angle (that of the V), make a cut in a slicing motion by lifting on the tool handle, thus making one side of the cut; repeat this for the other side, Fig. 42. If the V is large and deep, it will be necessary to make several cuts. Notice that the chisel is held high at the cutting edge when starting and lowered in the direction of the axis when finishing. Some turners prefer to use the toe, while others find that the heel works a little easier. Either way is correct and both work well, although a very deep narrow V is better made by using the toe.

The first steps in turning a bead are identical with those for the V, since V's are cut on either side of the bead, Fig. 43, to give clearance when making the final cuts.

To roll a bead, as it is commonly called, start with the ½"

·EXERCISE· OR· PRACTICE· PIECE·
·FOR·THE·BEGINNER·

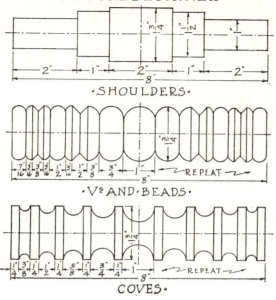

·SHOULDERS·

·Vˢ AND·BEADS·

COVES·

PLATE 1

skew chisel held at right angles to the axis, the cutting edge
high, and the tool flat upon the tee-rest, Fig. 44.

The point of the heel does all the cutting, and must therefore be very sharp and the bevel ground absolutely flat in order
to cut clean and with ease. Pivot the skew chisel over from a

FIGURE 44. Carefully note the position of the tool and hands when rolling
a bead. The heel of the chisel is used.

FIGURE 45. When cutting a cove, the gouge is held high and stood on its edge, then rolled over and the handle lowered.

horizontal position, lowering the cutting edge gradually by lifting on the handle, at the same time swinging the arm a little to one side. This completes one side or half the bead, provided the cut is deep enough and of the proper curvature. The other side is turned in like manner.

It is a good idea for beginners, in order to assure symmetry and to hold to the correct diameter, to mark a light pencil line on the center of each bead and cut to just a hair's breadth each side of this line.

Too much emphasis cannot be placed on the importance of keeping the bevel of the chisel flat at all times and the tool sharp. A rounded bevel is sure to cause trouble.

For very exacting work, and on wood that is difficult to turn, it is often advisable to scrape the bead rather than attempt to turn it by means of the cutting action of the skew chisel just described. In such cases, use a right and left hand skew scraper, Fig. 6. By whetting this tool occasionally (do not remove the burr that is formed), it is possible on hardwoods to make a fairly smooth and clean cut; then depend on sandpaper to do the final smoothing.

The Gouge Used for Turning Coves

The cove is generally conceded to be the most difficult form to cut. To some extent this difficulty is due to the fact that the gouge is the most difficult turning tool to sharpen properly.

The size gouge to use depends upon the size cove to be cut; for the general run of work, the ½″ gouge is used. Fig. 45 illustrates the making of the cut and shows the position of the gouge in the process of cutting a cove.

First lay out the size of the cove with a pencil. Begin to cut

38

FIGURE 46. The beginner will find it helpful, when turning a cove, to test it with a piece of dowel rod.

by holding the gouge flat on the tee-rest, and push gently into the wood to remove the most of the center portion. Now place the gouge on its edge, with the bevel at right angle to the axis of the wood and the handle of the tool held a bit high. Three motions are employed while making the cut: (1) Roll the gouge from a vertical to a horizontal position; (2) the handle is pried outward, forcing the cutting edge into the center; (3) the handle is held high when starting and lowered when finishing the cut.

It must be remembered that the cutting stroke each time stops in the center of the cove, and the gouge should not be worked up on the other side; otherwise the fibers of the wood will be torn, leaving the cove in a rough condition.

When turning a symmetrical cove, the beginner will find that it is desirable to test the cove by a gage or templet; several pieces of dowel rod of suitable diameters will serve the purpose very well, Fig. 46.

The novice will experience some difficulty at the start of turning a cove, first because the gouge is not ground flat on the bevel, and second because the bevel is not held at right angle to the axis of the wood. When these two instructions are overlooked, the gouge may travel along the wood and ruin the work.

For exacting work, especially on hardwood that is difficult to turn, a cove can be cut by using a round nose scraper, Fig. 6. Work as above from both sides.

Chapter Five

DESIGN IN WOOD TURNING

H AVING acquired the necessary skill in turning beads, coves, etc. (all of which make up any spindle project), and before actually attempting to turn a complete article, it will be well to carefully consider the subject of design in turning.

As the wood worker develops skill in turning, he is apt to show his ability unduly by turning a mass of beads and coves with no idea of creating a pleasing design.

The use to which we intend putting an article will, to a great extent, govern the general outline, proportion, etc. The character of the wood, whether simple or complex in grain, all helps to add to or detract from the design. A wood rich in grain often needs only a graceful turned outline to make it beautiful, the grain being the decorative feature.

A good design must have the following qualities: (1) simplicity, (2) unity, (3) variety, (4) harmony, and (5) good proportions.

Simplicity

Other things being equal, a simple article is the most beautiful. In working to this end, we must consider the profile— the general outline.

It must be remembered, however, that simplicity can lead to weakness in our design. There must be a certain amount of snap and strength to the work, not merely flowing lines.

The kind of line to use is of great importance. Too many straight lines must be avoided. Angular lines are ugly. The line of the circle is monotonous. So there remains only the line of variety and grace, and to this end we must work. Compare the line of a circle with that of a hen's egg. In the latter we have both grace and variety.

Unity

By unity is meant the holding together of all the parts to make the whole. Let there be a foundation line; to this all parts are to be subordinated. With unity we get balance—the balance of equal and unequal parts. The balance of equal parts can be shown by a dumbbell; here we have equal size units on both sides, hence perfect balance. Chair legs, candlesticks, and similar articles will show unequal balance. Here we have a large mass above and a small one below. In order to obtain good balance, when many parts are to be considered, it is necessary to group the parts and consider unity.

Variety

The line, it has been shown elsewhere, may have variety by changing its direction and thereby not obtaining the same curvature. The flowing line, as that of a bead turning into a cove—a compound curve—is continuous and often weak. In order to strengthen and add vigor and snap to such a curve, the fillet is often used (see darning ball project). Where a line comes to an abrupt end, and almost returns upon its own direction, we speak of it as contrasted; this should be avoided as much as possible. See the top of the potato masher.

Variety in decoration

When we add beads, coves, and fillets we must consider variety. All beads or all coves would be tiresome. Then, too, we must change the size of the beads and coves, not making all of them the same size.

Harmony

The design of the object must be in keeping with its use and one part with the other. A tall candlestick, for example, suggests solemnity and should be made rather slender. Of course, the diameter of the top portion must be sufficient to support the socket, and the base large enough to prevent the candle-

41

stick from being top-heavy. The base and the shaft should have some curve in common. In turning a gavel, it would not be advisable to turn a number of beads on the head, and only coves on the handle. One part should echo the other.

Proportion

Underlying the entire design we have the problem of proportion, and this, to a large extent, must be governed by common sense and usage. In order to gain strength, we must naturally increase the diameter and the thickness. This is brought out to some extent by the napkin ring. Since wood is not as strong as metal, our napkin ring must be kept a little heavier, and this applies to many other projects.

No one can hope to become expert in the art of wood turning without a real sense of appreciation for beauty in lines and forms, and without putting into his work a touch of artistic self-expression. You must not only be able to recognize a beautiful curve, but you must be able to reproduce that line of the drawing on the article you turn; you must develop a sensitive feeling in order to express yourself in objects of utility and beauty.

Chapter Six

DARNING BALL

THE darning ball will always be a useful and welcome article for the housewife to have in her sewing or mending basket. This was chosen for the first complete project, since it has a combination of the exercise cuts just explained in a proceeding chapter, and, in addition to this, the use of sandpapering on turned objects and polishing is introduced. Plate 2.

The stock should be maple, or a combination of maple and some dark wood such as ebony, Fig. 47. The dimensions are 2⅜″ x 2⅜″ x 9″. Maple or a combination of light and dark woods was chosen since most stockings and socks are dark or

FIGURE 47. The darning ball here shown is built-up of bird's-eye maple and ebony. A very useful article for the housewife and one that is easy to turn.

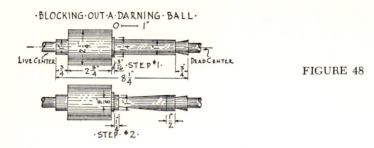

·BLOCKING·OUT·A·DARNING·BALL·

FIGURE 48

very light in color, which gives the mender a good opportunity to see where the hole is that requires darning; and, since the needle constantly rubs against the ball part, some hardwood is essential.

If you have decided to build up your stock of different woods, the utmost care must be exercised when planing the different pieces to get exactly the same thicknesses on both sides of the object; otherwise, when the project is turned, the figure will be quite different on the two sides, instead of identical.

Method of Procedure

Step 1

Turn to the largest diameter (allow a little for turning to the design shown), in this case $2\frac{5}{16}''$.

Step 2

Part down to $\frac{5}{8}''$ at the dead center end, and $1''$ at the live center end.

Step 3

Block out the job as shown, Fig. 48.

Step 4

With a $1''$ skew chisel, turn the left-hand end of the ball, then the right-hand end, thus clearing away enough wood so that the small bead and cove can then be turned.

44

Step 5

Next the tapered portion of the handle is shaped, working from the dead end in toward the center, so as to go in the direction with the grain of the wood. Finally, the rounded end of the handle is turned with a $\frac{1}{2}$" skew chisel. It will be safe now to cut away the waste wood at both ends to about $\frac{5}{16}$" in diameter, making an abrupt tapered cut so as not to strike the metal centers with your tool.

The project is now ready for sandpapering and then polishing; this will be taken up in the next chapter.

Step 6

After the darning ball has been properly finished (*while still in the lathe*), the waste wood of the ends is then cut off as follows: Remove the work from the lathe, saw off the waste wood quite close to the rounded ends, and then, with a sharp sloyd knife, trim up both ends; follow this with a good job of sandpapering so as to remove every scratch or mar. It may be necessary, while sandpapering, to take off some of the polish, but this can easily be refinished by hand.

·DARNING·BALL·

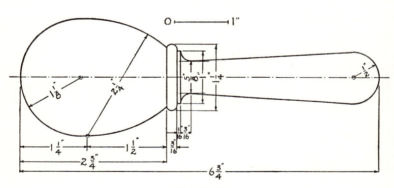

PLATE 2

45

Chapter Seven

SANDPAPERING IN THE LATHE

I<small>T GOES</small> without saying that the cleaner and smoother the piece is turned, the less sandpapering will be necessary. Be sure to complete all turning before starting to sandpaper; otherwise the small particles of grit from the paper will work their way into the pores of the wood, and, should it then be necessary to do any further turning, it will be difficult to keep a keen edge on the tools.

Garnet sandpaper is best to use, since it cuts cleaner and faster and will last longer; so in the long run it is the most economical, although costing a trifle more than flint paper.

The condition of your turning will determine what grade of paper to start with; in most instances, No. ½ or No. 0 will be found coarse enough. If not, then use No. 1. Long straight portions should be sandpapered by holding the paper between blocks; coves and beads and other curved parts are sanded by using small strips of paper and then very carefully shaping the portion being sandpapered, Fig. 50. Great care should be exercised not to round off the sharp corners of fillets or otherwise the character will be taken out of the project. Many a well turned job is entirely ruined by the careless use of sandpaper. On the other hand, it is possible to improve your poor turning by carefully sandpapering each part as a separate unit, and not merely slurring over the entire project. The coarse sandpaper will quickly remove the irregular places, but will badly scratch the wood. To remove these scratches, follow with the next finer grade of sandpaper, No. 0, then 2/0 and so on until all fine scratches have been removed, which may require using No. 7/0 paper. The sandpaper must be moved slowly back and forth

46

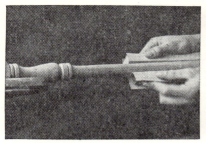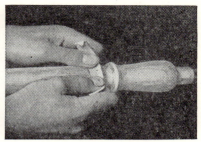

FIGURE 49. Long straight parts and slender pieces are best sandpapered by means of two blocks covered with sandpaper. Pressure is exerted at both top and bottom. FIGURE 50. Use small strips of sandpaper when sanding in a lathe. Great care must be exercised not to round off the sharp corners of the turning.

to avoid cutting rings on the wood. The final sandpapering is done with partially worn out paper.

It is impossible to produce a fine finish on a project that has been poorly sandpapered. The surface of the wood must be prepared as nearly perfect as possible, and this is emphasized by trying the following experiment:

Turn a piece of maple to a smooth surface; carefully sandpaper and then, instead of applying any finish whatsoever, simply polish the piece of maple by rubbing, in the lathe, with a smooth piece of soft wood such as pine. Care must be taken not to cause too much friction lest the wood become burnt. If this is worked carefully, a fairly high gloss will result. In other words, when the surface is made absolutely smooth and even, a gloss will appear.

When possible, it is advisable to sandpaper on the top of the turned piece, as this gives the turner a better chance to watch the work. Long straight work of small diameter should be sandpapered as shown, Fig. 49. The operator can bear down with the one hand and up with the other, giving support to the work and, at the same time, securing twice the cutting capacity.

When sandpapering the inside of a box (and this is doubly important for boxes with covers fitting on the inside), Plate 43, great care must be taken not to allow the sandpaper to drag over the edge, thereby wearing away too much of the neck of the box.

Small fillets, V's, etc., are often left without any sandpapering, as it is next to impossible to work with paper on such small surfaces.

Refer to Figs. 108 and 119 for special lathe sandpapering.

Chapter Eight

FINISHING

THE finishing of a project in the lathe differs from general cabinet work only in a few details. First of all, any article that has been stained must be set aside to dry thoroughly before it is allowed to rotate in the lathe; otherwise the centrifugal force will drive the stain out, instead of allowing it to penetrate into the wood. Secondly, when a project is to be rubbed down, this can often be easily accomplished in the lathe by simply *gently* bringing the rubbing felt and pumice powder in contact with the object as it revolves. Great care must be exercised not to apply too much pressure, or you will rub through the finish. If projects of several parts are to be finished in the lathe, they must be finished as separate pieces and assembled afterward.

The kind of finish you put on an object will depend on the wood used and the purpose the article is made for. All utensils for the kitchen or objects from which one eats, such as salad bowls, are not finished at all. Salad bowls are usually given a liberal coat of olive oil and then wiped dry; this prevents the oil of the salad dressing from penetrating the wood.

Generally speaking, three steps are taken in order to put a finish on a project: (1) staining, (2) filling, and (3) shellacking, lacquering, etc. If the wood is to be kept natural, no stain is required. When using close grained woods, such as maple, no filling is needed. To simplify matters, I will give specific directions for finishing most of the woods you will use, but I will first give directions on how to perform the different operations.

Staining

In most instances, water stains are to be preferred over oil or spirit stains. Water stains give a clear and more transparent color and penetrate deeper. In order to avoid lap marks, water stains must be applied very liberally. Small projects can be dipped and larger articles can be stained by spraying or by means of a brush. Usually it will be wiser to brush the stain on larger projects; this can be done in the lathe when the object is just a single piece. It will be found that water stain will raise the grain of the wood, which, however, is not a disadvantage, as will be seen further on. It is well to try out the stain for color on a scrap of the same kind of wood as the project is made of, to be sure of the final results. It is better to err on the side of staining too lightly and thus avoid a funereal effect which is often produced, especially when imitating mahogany. Always wipe the surplus stain off with a rag. Allow at least twenty-four hours for the stain to dry thoroughly.

Wash coat of shellac

Apply a brush coat of white shellac to the entire project. Mix the shellac *thin*, so that it will run off the brush freely like water. The purpose of this application is to stiffen the fibers of the wood that were raised by the use of the water stain, making sandpapering easier and more effective. This wash coat should dry in less than an hour if put on in an artificially heated shop. As a matter of fact, the room where the finishing is carried on should be dry, free from dust and draught, and have a temperature of about 70°.

Sanding down

Be sure the wash coat is dry; then use No. 7/0 garnet sandpaper and give the entire project a thorough sandpapering while the work revolves in the lathe, or by hand on assembled projects.

Shading

A certain amount of shading is desirable but should be done with the utmost care to avoid a blotchy effect. Use a partly worn piece of sandpaper, and gently rub the highlights to a lighter shade; this will add vigor and enhance the project.

Filling

All open grained woods should be given a coat of silica paste wood filler in a shade to go well with the stain used. The purpose of the filler is to seal up the pores and thereby bring every part of the wood to an even surface. The filler builds a good wearing surface, since it dries very hard and it brings out the grain of the wood. Follow the directions on the can.

Shellac, lacquer, oil, and wax

Many of the lighter colored woods are simply given a liberal coat of boiled linseed oil, and then French polished—that is, using shellac as the polishing agent, and boiled linseed oil as a lubricant. Make a ball of cheesecloth, apply a dab of shellac, fold over one thickness of the cheesecloth, and add a few drops of the linseed oil. While the work spins around in the lathe, this polishing pad is brought in contact with the piece, moving back and forth so as to coat the wood evenly, Fig. 51. If too much shellac has been applied, the cloth will stick or pull rather hard. On the other hand, if too much oil has been added, the polish can be rubbed off entirely by passing a dry finger over the work while the lathe is stationary. In either case, more of one or the other must be added. Should the polish be too thick and look streaky, simply take the same cloth and, by a little friction, burn the shellac and cause it to flow again, so that it can be run off the work entirely or be put on in a more even manner. French polishing is by far the quickest way of finishing, but does not wear well and on large surfaces is difficult to get on evenly.

A satisfactory and fairly quick finish can be obtained by applying three or four thin coats of white shellac. Allow ample time for each coat to dry hard; then lightly rub down each coat with No. 8/0 sandpaper and rub down the final coat with pumice stone powder and crude oil. For a duller finish, use fine steel wool in place of the pumice stone and oil.

The old masters often used beeswax alone for finishing. Melt

51

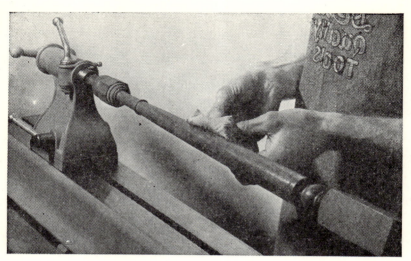

FIGURE 51. Applying French polish to a project.
The pad is worked back and forth.

down the wax on an electric heater (no gas or other flame) and, while it is hot, apply a brush coat; then, when it is hard, brush the wax vigorously with a soft brush.

For a good wearing finish, clear lacquer is best to use; this, however, must be applied with a sprayer (never use a brush). The first coat should be a sealing lacquer, which is applied after the stain, wash coat, and filler. Allow about twelve hours or more to dry hard; rub down with No. 7/0 garnet sandpaper; and then apply four or five spray coats of clear lacquer that has been thinned enough to work well in your spray gun. Build up sufficient body to the lacquer for the final rubbing, which is done with 3F pumice stone powder and crude oil. Be very careful to avoid runners or sags of lacquer while spraying. Allow four to five days for the final coat of lacquer to harden all the way through.

Some Special Finishes

Mahogany

Use either a water stain that you prepare yourself by dissolving the correct shade powder in water, or make up a saturated solution of bichromate of potash, diluted to shade desired. Follow directions given above for filling, etc.

Black walnut

Apply a wash coat of white shellac; then put on correct shade of wood filler, etc., as mentioned above.

Maple

Maple can be finished in a silver gray, amber, or many other colors by simply using the right color water stain. No filler is needed. Shellac and wax, or lacquer, as mentioned above.

Oak

Apply your favorite stain, filler, etc. For a rich brown effect, use a coat of bichromate of potash stain, filler, etc. For fumed oak, the correct way is to expose the wood to the fumes of strong ammonia in an airtight chamber; the chemical reaction of the fumes gives the wood the beautiful rich brown color so desirable. A good imitation of fumed oak can be secured by applying a ready-prepared stain.

Silver gray on oak and chestnut

Stain with oil walnut stain, using a dilute solution of one part to three parts turpentine. When dry, apply one coat of white wood filler (natural filler) or a thin coat of white oil paint. Rub off the surface at once while it is still wet. The white of the paint or filler will remain in the pores of the wood and also slightly coat the other part, giving that pleasing silvery effect. Follow with thin shellac, etc., as mentioned above.

Rare woods

The turner can often use to good advantage such woods as cocobolo, rosewood, ebony, lignum vitae, snakewood, Circassian walnut, myrtle, teak—in fact, any wood that is at all workable, regardless of gnarly places, etc., can be turned on the lathe and makes beautiful objects. To finish such woods, often

53

to bring out the natural beauty of the grain all that is necessary is to apply a liberal coat of boiled linseed oil and then follow directions given above for shellac, etc.

Shellac that is old often gives great trouble when finishing, so, for this reason, be sure that the shellac you purchase is fresh and is in a glass container. Buy only what you will need; do not store away shellac. For the thinner, use only the best denatured alcohol procurable.

White wood and birch

These woods are frequently used to imitate such woods as walnut and mahogany by using the correct color stain; then finish with shellac, etc., as directed above.

Chapter Nine

THINGS TO MAKE

The Potato Masher

ALTHOUGH called a potato masher, this is indispensable as a kitchen utensil; it can be used for making applesauce, cranberry sauce, and wherever food must be crushed and passed through a colander. Plate 3.

The stock should be hard maple, 2¾″ x 2¾″ x 12″. Follow either design. This is an ideal project for the beginner, as it is so simple to make. As with all similar articles, start with the largest diameter and work toward the small end.

·POTATO·MASHERS·

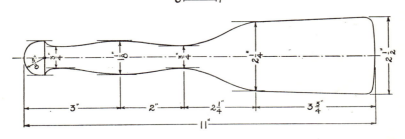

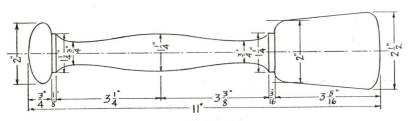

PLATE 3

No finish is to be applied to this project other than a thorough sandpapering, ending with No. 7/0 garnet sandpaper.

INDIAN CLUBS

This project offers an opportunity for the turner to try his skill by making a pair of Indian Clubs so that both will be alike, which, of course, is important to the person using them. By means of a templet, Fig. 52, it should be fairly easy to do this successfully. Plate 4.

The wood used in industry for Indian Clubs is maple; however, many other woods will serve equally well, but the clubs must be hard to give proper weight and also to withstand the hard usage given them. For those who like something a little out of the ordinary, stock for a pair of clubs can be built-up, using many different combinations of woods, Fig. 53. When doing this, however, great care must be exercised to have the pieces exactly the same thicknesses on both sides of the club, to assure symmetry of design in the completed project. The utmost care must also be taken when centering the rough stock.

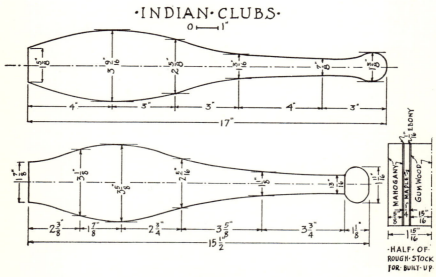

·INDIAN·CLUBS·

PLATE 4

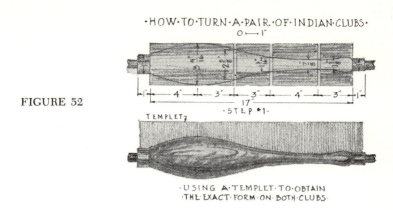

·HOW·TO·TURN·A·PAIR·OF·INDIAN·CLUBS·
0 ⊢——— 1"

FIGURE 52

·STEP #1·

TEMPLET

·USING·A·TEMPLET·TO·OBTAIN·
·THE·EXACT·FORM·ON·BOTH·CLUBS·

FIGURE 53. The Indian Clubs here shown are built-up of four different kinds of wood; the dumbbells are made of maple.

Stock for the solid one piece model is 3¾″ x 3¾″ x 19″; for the built-up design, 3⅞″ x 3⅞″ x 17″.

Method of procedure

1. Turn to largest diameter with the big gouge.

2. Part down for length and to exactly 1″ diameter at both ends. This is important, since the templet will rest on these two ends when the club has been turned to the correct design, which should then match the templet.

3. With a soft pencil, mark the distances where the different diameters are given on the drawing. Do *not* part down to these exact measurements, but allow a little for the final shaping.

4. Rough away the stock with a large gouge to conform *almost* to the design shown.

5. For a perfect fit, use the scraping chisels, Fig. 6, to do the final shaping of the club; again allow a trifle for sandpapering.

Now, while the lathe is stationary, set the templet in place so that you can see where more turning is necessary, if such should be the case.

6. Sandpaper with No. 1/2, 2/0, etc., and finally end with No. 7/0 garnet sandpaper. If you have succeeded, your pair of Indian Clubs will be a perfect match.

7. Finish in the lathe (see chapter on finishing). The work is then removed from the lathe and the ends cut off with a saw, trimmed to shape with a sharp sloyd knife, and finally sandpapered and finished by hand.

NOTE: After the club has been turned to match the templet, reduce the diameter of the waste wood at both ends so that the ball end can be shaped and the base slightly undercut.

Dumbbell

As with the Indian Clubs, maple is the commercial wood to use for making dumbbells. Plate 5.

Two methods can be successfully employed when turning this project. One is to use a templet having two semicircular portions and the handle design cut out; the second method

58

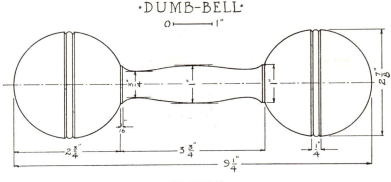

·DUMB-BELL·

PLATE 5

is to turn the ball ends by the aid of geometry. In either case, turn to the largest diameter and part down for the overall length and also the 2⅞″ length of each ball. The rough stock is 3″ x 3″ x 10¼″.

By the aid of geometry

Turn to a trifle over 2⅞″ and to 2⅞″ in length for each ball (as already mentioned). A section through the axis would then be a square. Now, with a soft pencil, lay off spaces so as to make an octagon (in section). With a skew chisel, cut off these 45° places, Fig. 54. Next, mark lines so that you will have a 16 sided polygon (in section); turn to these lines, then to 32, and, finally, 64 sides. It will be seen at once that by now the ball is almost formed. By removing the sharp corners, these end portions become nearly a perfect sphere.

It is advisable to lay out the circle of 2⅞″ on paper; then each time construct a square, octagon, etc., inside this circle. From this layout, you can get the exact measurements. The ones given on the drawing are approximate.

From geometry, we know that if we indefinitely increase the number of sides of a polygon, we approach a circle for the limit.

Having turned the two ball ends, the handle is shaped and finally the waste wood turned down to about ⁵⁄₁₆″ at both

59

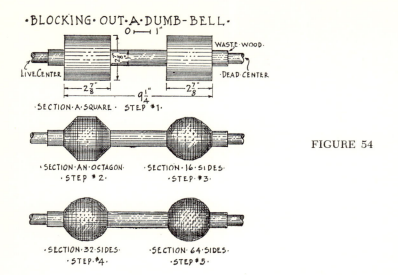

·BLOCKING· OUT·A·DUMB-BELL·

0 ⊢━━━┤ 1"

WASTE·WOOD·

LIVE·CENTER   ·DEAD·CENTER

←—2⅞"—→   ←—2⅞"—→

←————————— 9¼" —————————→

·SECTION·A·SQUARE· STEP·#1·

·SECTION·AN·OCTAGON·   ·SECTION·16·SIDES·
·STEP·#2·   ·STEP·#3·

·SECTION·32·SIDES·   ·SECTION·64·SIDES·
·STEP·#4·   ·STEP·#5·

FIGURE 54

ends. Apply the finish; then remove from the lathe, saw off the waste wood on the ends, and finish as with the Indian Clubs.

TOOL HANDLES

The craftsman is constantly confronted with the task of replacing broken tool handles or supplying handles for many of his hand tools, such as turning chisels, joiner's chisels, screw drivers, files, rasps, etc.

Almost any small scraps of hardwood work well for tool handles. Maple is generally used for the handles of chisels, although ash, hickory, and oak are very satisfactory. The hard, close grained woods are preferred, since there is less chance of splinters working into the hand. Plates 6, 7, and 8.

The method of procedure is much the same for all handles and differs only in minor details. Have the end for the ferrule (the small end) at the dead center. After shaping the handle to the design shown, carefully turn down the small end to fit the ferrule. This must be a tight fit, tight enough so that the ferrule must be forced on by light mallet taps.

Complete the turning of the handle with the ferrule in place. Sandpaper thoroughly; then finish with a coat of boiled linseed oil and finally a French polish (see finishing).

·SCREWDRIVER·HANDLES·

0 ⊢————⊣ 1"

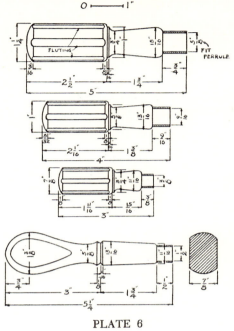

PLATE 6

·TURNING·TOOL·HANDLES·

0 ⊢————⊣ 1"

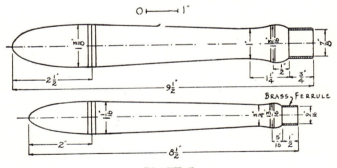

PLATE 7

When making a screw driver handle that is to be fluted, proceed as follows: With a pair of dividers, Fig. 55, step around the portion to be fluted, so as to lay off six equal dis-

61

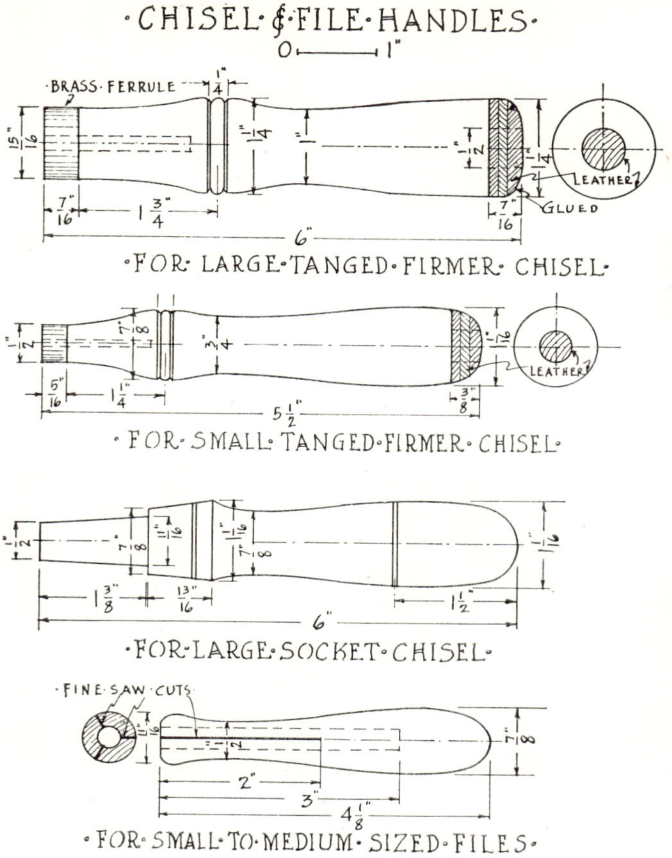
CHISEL & FILE HANDLES
BRASS FERRULE
LEATHER
GLUED
FOR LARGE TANGED FIRMER CHISEL
LEATHER
FOR SMALL TANGED FIRMER CHISEL
FOR LARGE SOCKET CHISEL
FINE SAW CUTS
FOR SMALL TO MEDIUM SIZED FILES

PLATE 8

tances. To do this, open the dividers to a measure equal to the radius of the cylinder. At each mark, draw a line. A simple way is to use the top edge of the tool rest, Fig. 56.

Use a small gouge to carve out the fluting, Fig. 57. Smooth these cuts by working a small piece of a rattail file back and forth; then follow this by sandpapering, Fig. 58. Wrap a small strip of sandpaper around a piece of the proper size dowel rod, and again work back and forth until the job has been made smooth. Of course, a far better way is to use a portable router, Fig. 123. *Do not* finish a fluted turned piece in the lathe.

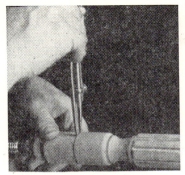 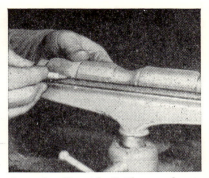

FIGURE 55. Stepping around a screw driver handle with dividers, to locate the fluting.

FIGURE 56. Using the tee-rest as a level guide, draw lines with a pencil for the fluting.

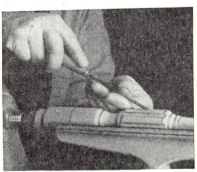 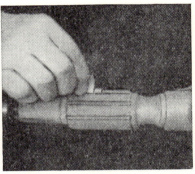

FIGURE 57. Carve out the fluting with a small gouge. FIGURE 58. The final smoothing of the fluting is done by wrapping a piece of sandpaper around a short length of the proper size dowel rod and then working this back and forth.

FIGURE 59

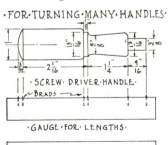

·FOR·TURNING·MANY·HANDLES·

·SCREW· DRIVER·HANDLE·

·GAUGE·FOR· LENGTHS·

· GAUGE· FOR·DIAMETERS·

63

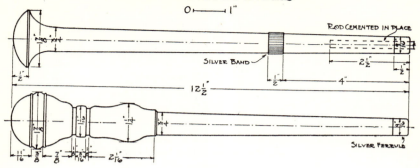

·UMBRELLA·HANDLES·

PLATE 9

The design showing the handle with flat portions must be turned from stock ⅞″ x 1½″; then, as the job is turned, the flat portions will shape up as shown.

Holes to receive the metal shank of the tool can easily be bored in the lathe, Figs. 66 and 67.

When turning a large number of screw driver handles, the little gage shown in Fig. 59 will save much time and make for accuracy. Plate 9.

KITCHEN TOWEL RACK

Every kitchen should be equipped with a towel rack; the one shown here has four bars—one for holding a towel for drying glasses and silver, two for the general run of dishes and pots and pans, and the fourth for a hand towel. If you use, as you should, a rack for draining the wet dishes, three towels will be sufficient for the average family. My wife has used a towel rack of this kind for many years and would not be without it. Plate 10.

The bars are turned between centers. The remaining part of the project is so elementary that I feel no further instructions are necessary.

Use maple for this rack and finish in paint and enamel in a color to suit your fancy. Fasten this towel rack near the kitchen sink and each day after the dinner dishes have been washed and dried, and the dish towels washed, this rack will be very

64

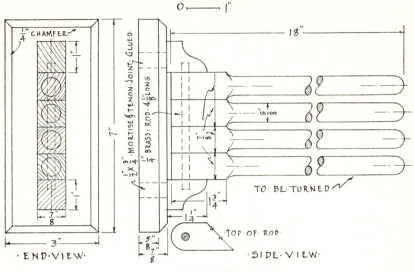

PLATE 10

convenient to hang the towels on for drying, clean and fresh for another day's usage.

MALLET

Lignum vitae is the best wood for a mallet head, Plate 11, although other kinds of hardwoods serve fairly well too.

The turning of a mallet is indeed a simple job. The only part needing great care and attention is the boring of the hole in the head and then fitting the handle to that hole.

In order that the hole in the head may be at right angles to the axis, and true in every direction, it is necessary to locate the center of this hole with the greatest accuracy. To do this, follow these simple directions: While the wood is in the lathe, and before sandpapering, mark the center line around the head with a soft pencil. The next step is to cross this line in two places, so that a line passing through these two points will be at right angles to the axis. Set the surface gage so that its point will coincide with the point on either the live or dead center (removing the wood, of course, in order to set the gage).

65

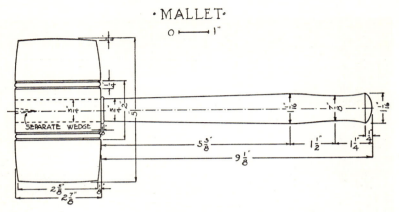

· MALLET·

PLATE 11

Place the wood back in the lathe, tightening on the tail-stock adjustment so that the wood cannot turn; hold the surface gage flat on the bed of the lathe and scribe a mark crossing the center line of the mallet head.

Do the same thing on the opposite side, not disturbing the adjustment of the surface gage, Fig. 60. The two points thus obtained are the required centers for the holes to be bored. In the absence of a surface gage, cut a piece of wood so that it will reach from the base of the lathe to exactly the center of the pins on either live or dead center ends and proceed as described above. Still another way, but not quite as good a one, is to step the radius of the mallet head six times around on the center line. Any two opposite points will be the centers.

Having carefully located the necessary points, make a deeper impression with a pair of dividers or scratch awl; then sandpaper and finish. If a chuck is available for boring in the lathe, place the point of the dead center into one of these holes (mentioned above) and the power auger bit, Fig. 61, or the drill with chuck into the other. Fasten the tailstock securely to the bed of the lathe, and while the left hand holds the mallet head, the right hand turns the spindle adjustment and forces the wood against the drill, thus boring the hole. Care must be taken to use a fairly high speed, and not to force the wood too much; otherwise the bit or drill will become very hot and lose

66

FIGURE 60. The surface gage is used to locate the two opposite points for boring holes to receive the handle of a mallet.

its temper. If you intend using an ordinary auger bit, first strip the threads off the screw end of the bit (with a file). If you do not do this, the bit will pull too quickly into the wood and may cause an accident. When the hole is almost through, remove the dead center, butting the head of the mallet against a scrap block of wood, so that you can bore all the way through without ruining the dead center pin.

By means of a V block and drill press, it is also easy to bore

·POWER·AUGER·BIT

FIGURE 61

67

the hole; and, of course, hand boring can be resorted to if necessary. Carefully turn the handle down to fit snugly into the mallet head. Make a saw cut in the end of the handle, so that when gluing the mallet together a wedge can be forced into the end, thereby spreading it slightly apart and assuring a permanent fit. It is advisable to make the handle a little long at the small end so that it can be cut to the exact length after it has been glued in place.

Bridge Novelty Pencil Holder

If you play bridge, canasta, or any other card game in which the score must be kept, you will find this little novelty

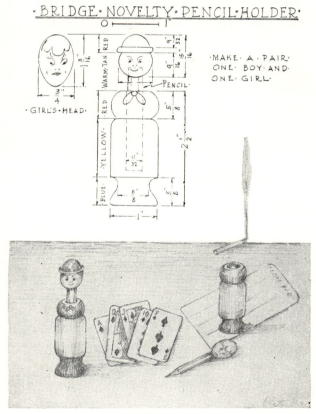

PLATE 12

very handy to have. It is unique, attractive, and will amuse your friends. Plate 12.

Use any fairly hard wood for this project; turn as one unit between centers, allowing about ⅜″ between the body part and the head piece so that you can cut in two pieces after the turning has been completed.

The hole in the head and body are bored either by hand or in your lathe or drill press.

Apply a thin coat of shellac to the entire job; when dry, sandpaper; then follow with one coat of enamel undercoating and one coat of gloss enamel. Follow the colors indicated.

GAVELS

Since a gavel is used to strike a blow, thereby making a loud sound, especially when struck against a hardwood surface, the wood must possess sonorous qualities. During periods of excitement, it is often necessary to use a gavel quickly and little

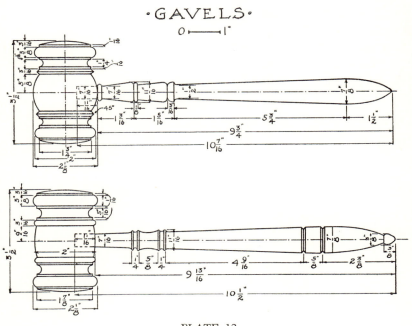

·GAVELS·

PLATE 13

69

attention is paid to where the gavel strikes; hence the ends must be well rounded. To meet these necessary requirements, a wood such as rosewood, cocobolo, or ebony serves best.

The stock for the head is $2\frac{1}{4}''$ x $2\frac{1}{4}''$ x $4\frac{1}{2}''$. Rough down to the largest diameter, cut to length (leaving the same amount of waste wood at each end), locate the center line with a soft pencil, and, on both sides of this line, lay off the work. At this point, it will be advisable to locate the center for boring the hole in the head; do this by marking a place with a scratch awl or the point of the dividers.

When turning a cove having a fillet at each side, it is advisable at first to ignore the cove entirely until the fillets have been cut clean; then work out the cove.

Before cutting the work free, bore the hole in the head for the handle. This should be done in the lathe, the work being clamped between centers as shown, Fig. 62.

The handle should be turned with the small end at the dead center. All parts are finished before fitting the handle into the head, so that no oil from the polish will reach the dowel part. On all work with one part which fits into another, bore the hole first; then fit the other part to that hole.

When the ends have been cleaned off, glue the handle into the head. Should the handle fit rather loosely, make a saw kerf

FIGURE 62. While it is held between centers, bore a hole in the gavel head to receive the handle.

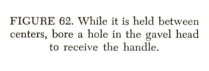

70

in the end, about ½″ down the handle, and, while gluing, force a wedge into this cut, thereby spreading the wood apart and assuring a tight fit.

Finish with boiled linseed oil and a French polish. Fig. 63.

THE ROLLING PIN

The rolling pin, Plate 14, like all wooden kitchen utensils, is made of maple, because maple does not sliver, is hard, and holds its shape well.

To make it easier to understand, this project will be divided into two parts—the shaft and the handles.

·ROLLING·PIN·

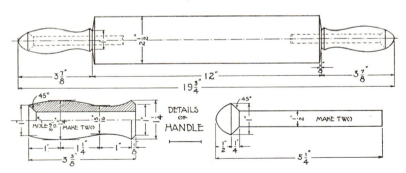

PLATE 14

71

The shaft

The stock for the shaft is $2\frac{5}{8}''$ x $2\frac{5}{8}''$ x $12\frac{1}{4}''$. Turn to $2\frac{1}{2}''$ diameter and cut to length, leaving the waste wood at each end $1''$ in diameter. Now cut the taper on both ends by using the point of a sharp $1''$ skew chisel. The cut is started $\frac{1}{8}''$ back from the edge of the stock, and ends at the $1''$ diameter of the waste wood. After the job has been thoroughly sandpapered, remove from the lathe and cut off the waste wood. At each end, the lathe centers have left a small hole which will serve as the centers when boring for the handles.

The ends are easily bored absolutely true by using a chuck in the lathe, or on a drill press. You will find it quite difficult to do this accurately by hand. It is very important that these holes be bored true; otherwise the handles will not revolve as they should.

The handles

In order to have the hole of the handle in the exact center, bore the hole first and then turn around this hole, Fig. 64. To do this, take a piece of maple $1\frac{1}{2}''$ x $1\frac{1}{2}''$ x $4\frac{1}{2}''$; bore a $\frac{9}{16}''$ hole all the way through. Do this on two pieces. Now turn two separate pieces of stock to a trifle over $1''$ in diameter and $6''$ long. Measure $1\frac{1}{4}''$ from the live center end and then for the remaining $4\frac{3}{4}''$ turn down to $\frac{9}{16}''$ in diameter so as to fit the hole bored in the other pieces. Glue $\frac{1}{4}''$ of this piece at both ends to the piece with the hole in it. When the glue has set hard, turn the handle portion to the design and sandpaper. Refer to the drawing for further help.

Use a $\frac{1}{8}''$ chisel and make the 45° cut at one end; this will then cut that end free. Cut away the waste wood at the other end, thereby making second end free. Remove handle part.

The spindle portion of the handle is now completed by shaping the large end and turning down the rest to fit the $\frac{1}{2}''$ hole bored in the shaft. Do not sandpaper the end that is to be glued in place. Put the two parts of the handle together and then place in the lathe. Shape and sandpaper the end to a smooth continuous line. It will be necessary to wedge the handle portion in place temporarily while doing this.

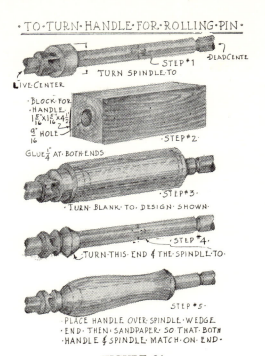

·TO·TURN·HANDLE·FOR·ROLLING·PIN·

DEAD CENTER

STEP #1
TURN SPINDLE TO

LIVE CENTER

·BLOCK·FOR·
·HANDLE·
$1\frac{5}{16}" \times 1\frac{5}{16}" \times 4\frac{1}{2}"$
$\frac{9"}{16}$ HOLE

·STEP #2·

GLUE $\frac{1}{4}"$ AT·BOTH·ENDS

·STEP #3·
·TURN·BLANK·TO·DESIGN·SHOWN·

·STEP #4·
·TURN·THIS·END OF THE·SPINDLE·TO·

STEP #5·
PLACE HANDLE OVER SPINDLE WEDGE
·END·THEN·SANDPAPER·SO·THAT·BOTH
·HANDLE OF SPINDLE·MATCH·ON·END·

FIGURE 64

When gluing the handle to the shaft, great care must be exercised not to allow any glue to get into the hole of the handle, and also not to force the handle up too tight against the shaft.

If you have followed these detailed directions and sketches, you will have turned out a perfect rolling pin, Fig. 65.

FIGURE 65. This ideal rolling pin is unsurpassed for making pies and wherever dough must be rolled out.

Lathe Boring

For accuracy, speed, and ease, the lathe offers one of the best ways of boring a hole in wood.

The instructions here given are general, and apply to many of the projects shown in this book. When boring a hole in a mallet head or similar job, it is advisable first to start the hole by hand with an auger bit and brace, to make sure of the correct location. The point of the dead center takes care of the other end. Having located the correct distance the tailstock should be from the drill, to allow for the size of the wood to be bored, fasten the tailstock firmly in place, but leave the spindle free. Working at a medium speed, force the wood against the drill or bit by turning on the spindle adjustment, Figs. 66 and 67. When the hole has been bored almost through the object, remove the dead center and butt the hollow spindle against the wood to allow the bit or drill to go all the way through without injury to the center. For large holes, butt against scrap wood. This method can also be used on end grain boring on the rolling pin handles. When a hole is to be bored longer than the length of the bit at hand, simply reverse the piece being bored and bore halfway from each end, or forge on a rod to lengthen the bit or drill.

When feeding the drill into the wood, it is wise to pull the bit out now and then to clean out the shavings that accumulate and also to cool off the bit. It often becomes necessary to cool the bit, if it is too hot, by dipping in cold water.

For faceplate boring, where there is danger of splitting the

FIGURE 66. A rapid accurate hole can be bored, as shown, in a lathe. The wood is forced into the bit by simply turning on the dead-center spindle.

74

FIGURE 67. The power auger bit is used for all kinds of lathe boring; it cuts a clean hole very rapidly. The bit is held in a chuck and placed in the headstock of the lathe; the left hand holds the wood from revolving, while the right hand forces the wood into the bit by turning on the end spindle.

wood, it is advisable to use a Foerstner bit, since the screw on the auger bit is very apt to force the wood apart and, of course, the hole made by the screw part of the bit might show on the good side of the project. If an ordinary auger bit must be used, then file off the screw threads first, so as to prevent the bit from pulling too fast and causing injury. In order to center a Foerstner bit, turn in a short distance first with a chisel. A center bit is also good to use for certain jobs. Refer to Figs. 61 and 67, which show an excellent type of power auger bit for lathe and drill press boring.

COLONIAL MIRROR

This mirror frame, Plate 15, is fashioned after the old Colonial frames at one time so generally used throughout the New England Colonies and which are again rapidly gaining in popularity.

Make a simple frame out of ¾″ stock, 18″ x 26″ in size, halved together at the corners and rabbeted on the back as show on the detail. Use any good quality of straight grain wood for this frame, or, if you prefer, a choice hardwood.

75

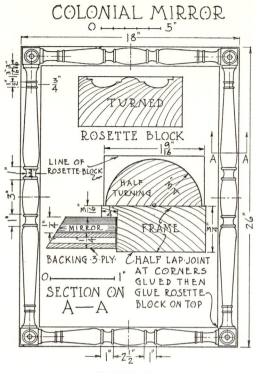

COLONIAL MIRROR

TURNED

ROSETTE BLOCK

LINE OF
ROSETTE·BLOCK

HALF
TURNING

MIRROR   FRAME

BACKING·3·PLY·   HALF LAP·JOINT
                AT CORNERS
SECTION ON   GLUED THEN
   A—A   GLUE ROSETTE
                BLOCK ON TOP

PLATE 15

The corner rosettes are turned on a screw chuck, Fig. 68. Use square stock 1″ thick and 1⁹⁄₁₆″ square. Turn to the design shown.

The turned facing of the frame is done by what is known as split turning—that is, either the stock is glued together with a heavy piece of paper in between the two pieces of wood, or the stock is simply held together at both ends with screws, Fig. 69.

Since only half pieces are used, it will be necessary only to turn one long and one short piece. After the job has been turned and sandpapered, the glued pieces are split apart on the glued line with a broad chisel.

Gently tap the chisel with a mallet. Do this in several places and from both sides of the job. After the pieces have been

76

FIGURE 68. Faceplate. Bell chuck. Screw chuck.

separated, remove the glue and paper with a cabinet scraper or chisel and coarse sandpaper.

To assemble, first glue the foundation frame together and, when the glue has set, clean up this frame with a plane. Now glue the rosette blocks in place, and finally the turned members.

Many of the old frames were either finished entirely by gilding, or the foundation part was finished in black enamel and the turned members gilded. This, however, is a detail for the craftsman to determine for himself. If the frame is to be gilded, use any close-grained wood; otherwise, curly maple, finished in an antique effect, or, as a matter of fact, any good cabinet wood to suit your choice, will be satisfactory.

If the frame is to be gilded, it must be prepared in the following manner: Sandpaper the work thoroughly; then brush off all dust. Apply a coat of hot size of one part rabbit's-skin

FIGURE 69

·SPLIT·TURNING·

·GLUE· TOGETHER· WITH· ·HEAVY· PAPER· IN· JOINT·

COUNTERSINK

· HOLD· PIECES· TOGETHER· ·WHILE· TURNING· WITH· SCREWS·

77

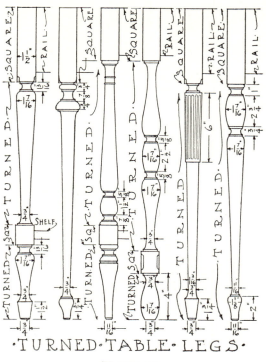

·TURNED·TABLE·LEGS·

PLATE 16

glue and one part water. (Glue is taken from a stock mixture made up of 1½ oz. glue, 10 oz. water, and one teaspoonful carbolic acid.) Or, in place of the glue size, use thin shellac. When it is dry, rub down thoroughly; then apply several coats of a mixture of warm but not hot whiting and glue. Sandpaper and then apply a coat of burnish gold size, and finally the gold or bronze powder, whichever you prefer to use. The highlights are burnished.

Table Legs

Turned table legs, in place of the plain square ones, add much to any project. The group here shown gives a good variety which, with some variations, should be suitable for almost any table you wish to construct. Plate 16.

When the design calls for a section to be left square, that

78

·BLOCKS·GLUED·ON·LEG·TO·BE·
·TURNED· TO ·GIVE·EXTRA·THICKNESS·

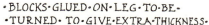

GLUE · IN·TWO·
OPERATIONS·

FIGURE 70

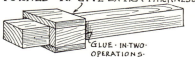

· BALUSTERS & NEWEL ·

0 ———— 5"

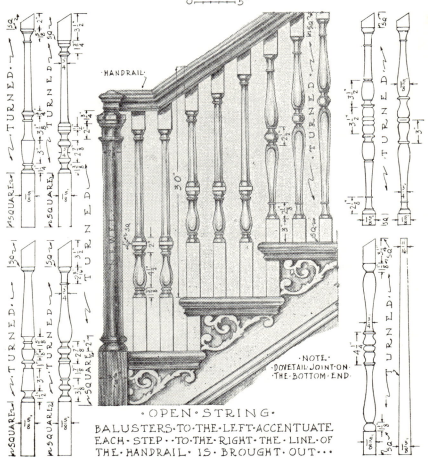

·HANDRAIL·

·NOTE·
·DOVETAIL·JOINT·ON·
·THE·BOTTOM·END·

·OPEN·STRING·
BALUSTERS·TO·THE·LEFT·ACCENTUATE
EACH·STEP· ·TO·THE·RIGHT·THE·LINE·OF
THE·HANDRAIL· IS·BROUGHT·OUT···

PLATE 17

part should be laid out first on the square stock by squaring lines around the wood. Great care must be exercised when turning, not to chip off these sharp corners, Fig. 70.

BALUSTERS AND NEWEL

The staircase lends itself to unlimited opportunities for artistic expression. It would be out of the scope of this book to attempt to cover this problem completely; nevertheless, since turned balusters and newels play so important a part, I will give two plates, one showing the open string and the other the closed string type. Plates 17 and 18.

Much of this information has been gathered from the fine old Colonial staircases that have been handed down to us.

As the height of the riser and length of the tread must be determined by each special staircase, the overall length of balusters will have to be omitted. Furthermore, the type staircase you prefer and the number of balusters to use for each step must be determined by you.

For the open string type, you will notice that I show designs for two entirely different balusters. The one to the left accentuates the horizontal tread having the top of the lower square section parallel with the tread, and all turned members are the same height. To the right, the turned members are parallel with the slope of the handrail, which suggests speed of motion. Both types are very effective.

The number of balusters to use for each step is first determined by the width of the tread and the effect desired. All balusters should be fastened to the tread by a dovetail joint nailed and glued in place. The tenon part can be roughed off on the lathe. For cheap work, dowel ends are turned in place of the dovetail. Care must be taken when turning, to hold the sharp square corners where shown.

In order to obtain the overall length of the balusters (note three different lengths), it is advisable to make a full size layout showing one step and the slop of the handrail with, of course, the balusters.

Newel posts are usually made simpler in design and must be quite heavy for a rigid job.

·BALUSTERS·

0 ⊢——⊣ 5"

·CLOSED·STRING·
LATE·17ᵀᴴ ℰ EARLY 18ᵀᴴ CENTURY·ENGLISH
ALSO·EARLY·AMERICAN···USED·NOW·

PLATE 18

Turned Finials

Finials placed on fence and gate posts, entrances, cabinets, clock cases, and many other pieces of furniture often add that much needed finishing touch to the project. Fig. 71.

81

FIGURE 71. This turned finial, carved to imitate a torch, is made of curly maple and used on a mirror frame.

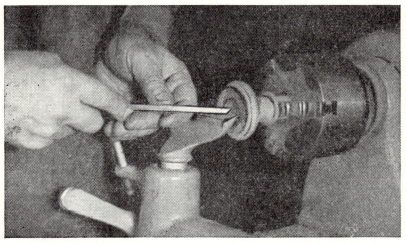

FIGURE 72. The universal chuck is indispensable for holding drawer knobs and the like, while you are turning the end to design.

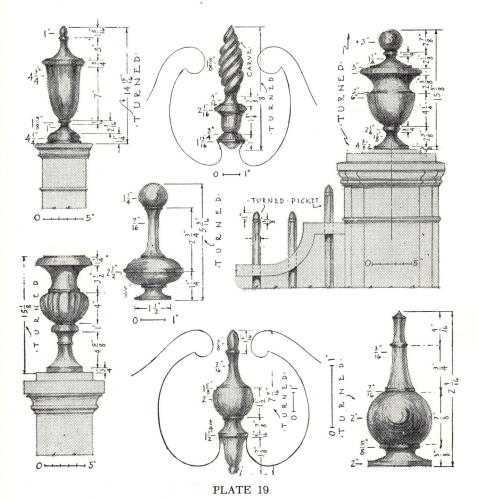

PLATE 19

Use a good grade of clear white pine, cypress, red cedar, California redwood, or plain Mexican mahogany for finials to be used outdoors, as these woods will withstand the elements of the weather best. For objects to be used indoors, any good workable wood will be satisfactory.

All the largest finials are turned entirely between centers and are therefore simple to make. Some of the smaller ones

83

may have to be turned partly by the aid of a universal chuck, Fig. 72, Plate 19.

COLONIAL FOOTSTOOL

If you would like a good place to rest your tired feet, I can recommend this simple yet attractive footstool, to be made out of some odds and ends of choice hardwood.

The legs are done with simple spindle turning; care must be exercised not to chip off the square corners. The holes for the dowel joints can be bored in the lathe. Assemble in two separate operations. Make a separate frame to hold the upholstery. The corner blocks will do much to stiffen the entire job. Plate 20, Figs. 73 and 74.

TURNED BENCH

This useful and attractive piece of furniture can be made

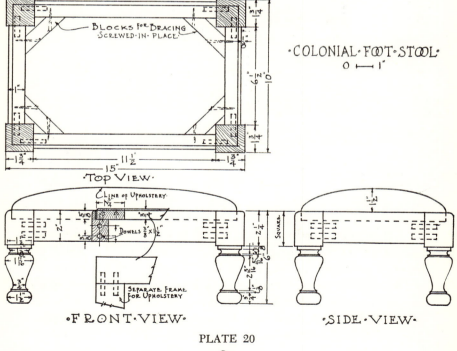

·COLONIAL·FOOT·STOOL·

·TOP VIEW·

·FRONT·VIEW·

·SIDE·VIEW·

PLATE 20

FIGURE 73. This handy and efficient dowel cutter is like a big pencil sharpener. The one shown is for making the smaller size dowels, ⅛″ to ½″.

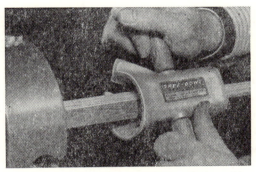

FIGURE 74. With this model, dowels from 9/16″ to 1¼″ in diameter can quickly be cut on the lathe. If your chuck is equipped with but three jaws, then first round up the end for a short distance to properly center the stock to be cut.

almost entirely on a lathe; it will be a welcome addition to any living room, Fig. 75.

Maple, mahogany, walnut, or other fairly hard wood should be used for the turned part. Use any sound scrap material for the top rails, as the upholstery will cover them.

Be careful when turning, to hold the sharp corners of the square portions. To do this, pencil lines are squared around the stock before starting to turn; then, when turning, take a light cut each time and be sure the tool is sharp.

FIGURE 75. The turned bench, as its name implies,
can be made almost entirely on a lathe.

When finishing, be sure to bring out the highlights to add
life and vigor to this project. Plate 21.

This piece should be upholstered with springs. In my book
KLENKE'S FURNITURE BOOK, simple complete directions for doing this upholstery work are given.

CRICKET

This charming little old Colonial project should be made
out of some hardwood such as maple, birch, or beech. Since
only small pieces are required, use up some of your short odds
and ends of choice stock that accumulate around the shop.

The turned parts are very simple to make and the top can
be cut out on the band saw; then shape the edge by hand or on
a shaper. Assemble in one operation. Finish in an antique effect. Plate 22.

FOLDING LUGGAGE STAND

This folding luggage stand serves not only for holding luggage when your week-end guests arrive, but also makes an ex-

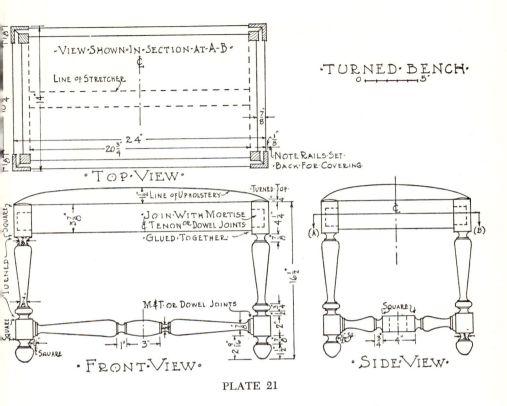

·VIEW·SHOWN·IN·SECTION·AT·A·B·

LINE OF STRETCHER

·TURNED·BENCH·

24"

20¾"

·NOTE·RAILS·SET·
·BACK·FOR·COVERING·

·TOP·VIEW·

IN LINE OF UPHOLSTERY
·TURNED·TOP·

JOIN·WITH·MORTISE
& TENON OR DOWEL JOINTS
·GLUED·TOGETHER·

M.&T. OR DOWEL JOINTS

TURNED SQUARE

SQUARE

SQUARE

·FRONT·VIEW·

(A)

(B)

SQUARE

·SIDE·VIEW·

PLATE 21

cellent tray stand when serving coffee or tea in the living room, on the porch, or out on the lawn.

This project calls for simple spindle turning; the legs are held together at the center with rivets, while upholsterer's webbing is fastened across the top; or, if you prefer, use some other tough, attractive material, such as striped denim.

If you intend using this stand in some special room, I would then select a wood to match the remainder of the furniture in that room. When folded up, this stand can be tucked away in a very small space. Plate 23.

Drawer Knobs, Rosettes, and Caster Cups

Drawer knobs are sometimes turned between centers, with a dowel end for gluing, or turned out of flat stock on a screw

87

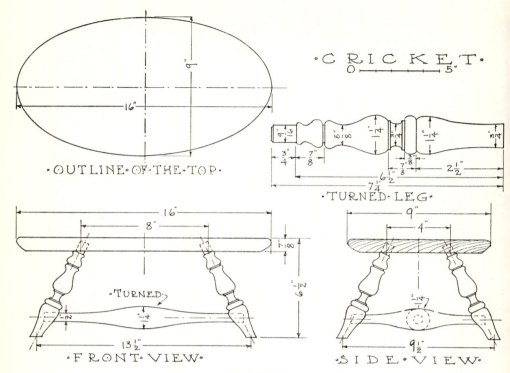

·OUTLINE·OF·THE·TOP·

·CRICKET·
0 ————————— 5"

·TURNED·LEG·

·TURNED·

·FRONT·VIEW·

·SIDE·VIEW·

PLATE 22

chuck, Fig. 68. It all depends on the size of the knob to be turned and on what furniture or object it is to be used, which method you employ. Plate 24.

When turning between centers a knob that has an intricate top face, all turning is first done in the regular manner except for the top face; this is then turned by placing the dowel end in the jaws of a universal chuck for a grip to hold the work; then do the turning on the top end, Fig. 72.

Drawer knobs that are turned out of flat stock are either handled on a screw chuck or the wood is glued to scrap stock first, with paper between, and fastened to a small faceplate. Your individual problem will determine which method is best to use.

Rosettes are always handled as faceplate or screw chuck

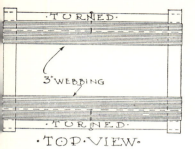

·TURNED·

3" WEBBING

·TURNED·

·TOP·VIEW·

·FOLDING·LUGGAGE·STAND·

0 |—|—|—|—|—| 5"

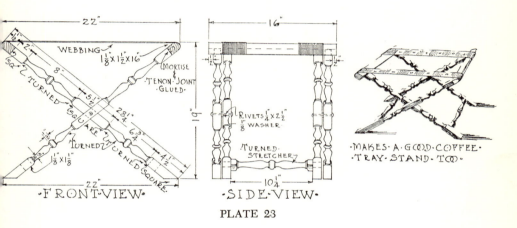

— 22" —

WEBBING
1⅛"x1½"x16"

8"

·SQ.·

TURNED

·CARE·

5"

28¼"

6¾"

TURNED

·CARE·

TURNED

1⅛"x1⅛"

TURNED·SQUARE·

4½"

MORTISE
&
·TENON·JOINT·
·GLUED·

— 22" —

·FRONT·VIEW·

— 16" —

RIVETS ¼"x2½"

⅛" WASHER

·TURNED·
STRETCHER

10¼"

·SIDE·VIEW·

·MAKES·A·GOOD·COFFEE·
·TRAY·STAND·TOO·

PLATE 23

turning. The blank stock is glued to scrap stock with paper between. Turn in the usual manner.

Caster cups are indispensable for placing under the legs of heavy pieces of furniture to prevent the caster from cutting its way through your carpet or rug.

The making of a caster cup is the same as the directions given for turning a nut bowl.

BOWLS

Bowls and trays come under the heading of faceplate work, and, regardless of design, are all worked out in much the same manner. However, to make the following description a little easier to understand, we will take one of the nut bowls for our example. Plate 25.

The rough stock should be 1⅜″ x 4¾″ x 4¾″, dressed on

89

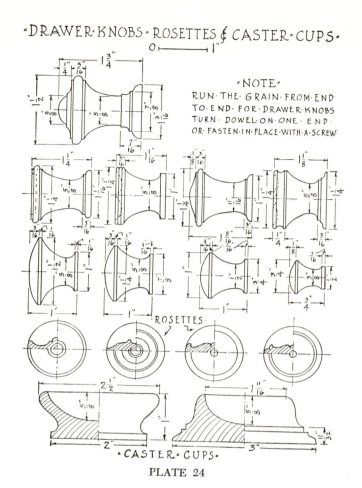

·NOTE·
RUN·THE·GRAIN·FROM·END
TO·END·FOR·DRAWER·KNOBS
TURN·DOWEL·ON·ONE·END·
OR·FASTEN·IN·PLACE·WITH·A·SCREW·

·ROSETTES·

·CASTER·CUPS·

PLATE 24

one face. Cut out a 4¾″ circle on the band saw. If no band saw
is available, simply cut off the corners with a handsaw. Glue
the dressed surface to a piece of scrap stock (whitewood or
pine is good), of about the same diameter, with a piece of
heavy paper between. The object of the paper is to separate
the fibers of the waste wood from the wood to be turned, so
that a few light taps with a chisel and mallet will separate the
two pieces when the turning has been completed, Fig. 80.

After the glue has set, screw the faceplate on the scrap
stock. Start the lathe at slow speed, with the tool rest parallel

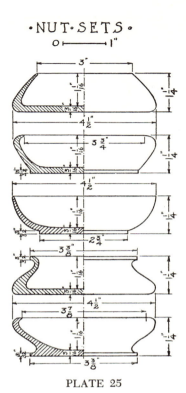

PLATE 25

with the face of the work and a *trifle* below the center line. By means of the ⅛″ mortising chisel, held horizontally and standing on its edge, cut in the direction indicated, Figs. 76 and 77.

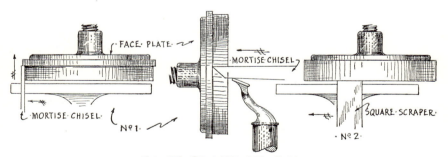

·FACE·PLATE·WORK·

FIGURE 76

91

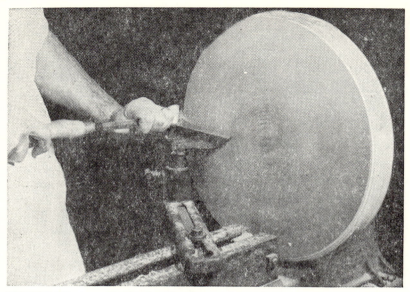

FIGURE 77. A gap-bed lathe like the one here shown permits turning quite large stock. The outside of the wood is first trued up by holding an ⅛″ mortising chisel or parting tool on its edge when making the cut.

Do not cut the entire thickness of the stock; otherwise the wood on the opposite face will split off. Merely cut off enough wood to center the work. Now turn the tool rest parallel with the edge of the stock, and, using a flat scraper, clean off the small remaining portion of the wood.

Having turned the wood to the largest possible diameter, face off the surface with a 1″ flat scraper, always working from the center out. Cut the stock down to 1¼″ thick, measured from the glued joint.

Make a full size drawing of the bowl, showing, as I have, the profile of both the outside and line of the inside. Now make a cardboard pattern of one half of the inside, Fig. 78. Cut this out with scissors and use it as your templet.

With a ⅛″ mortising chisel, cut a diameter of about 1″ and to a depth of 1¹⁄₁₆″ (scant measurement). Measure the depth as shown, Fig. 79. Hollow out the inside of the bowl with a round-nose scraper, to conform with the templet. Now sandpaper thoroughly. Shape the outside with flat, skew, and

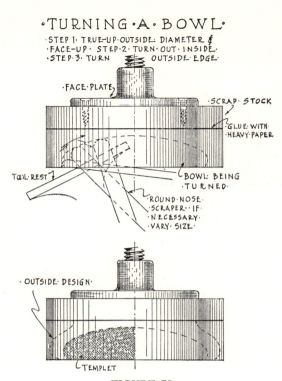

·TURNING·A·BOWL·
·STEP 1· TRUE-UP·OUTSIDE· DIAMETER &
·FACE-UP· STEP·2· TURN·OUT·INSIDE.
·STEP·3· TURN   OUTSIDE·EDGE·

·FACE·PLATE·

·SCRAP· STOCK

·GLUE· WITH·
·HEAVY· PAPER·

TOOL·REST·

·BOWL· BEING·
·TURNED·

·ROUND·NOSE·
·SCRAPER·· IF·
·NECESSARY·
·VARY· SIZE·

· OUTSIDE· DESIGN·

TEMPLET

FIGURE 78

round-nosed scrapers, keeping the thickness as shown on the drawing. Caliper this thickness with your fingers. Having performed all necessary turning of the outside, sandpaper thoroughly; then finish. See Chapter Eight.

FIGURE 79. Using a chisel as a straightedge, held against the face of the bowl, the depth of the inside is measured.

FIGURE 80. To cut the bowl free from the scrap stock, put a broad chisel in the glued joint and tap with a mallet as shown.

To separate the bowl from the waste wood, place a broad chisel (joiner's tool) in the glued joint. With the bevel against the waste wood, tap gently with a mallet in several places.

It will be well to place a small bundle of waste or rags on the lathe bed directly under the turned project, so that the finish is not marred on the bowl as it drops down, Fig. 80.

If you have a sanding disk, simply wear off the glue on the bottom of the bowl by placing it against the disk, or scrape it off by hand. Then glue on a piece of felt, using hot glue or shellac. If shellac is used, first apply a coat of shellac to the wood. When it is dry, apply another rather liberal coat of shellac, and, when this becomes tacky to the touch, apply the felt. Trim off the edge of the felt with a sharp knife after the shellac is dry.

Nut Set

A nut set should include a large nut bowl and six or eight small bowls, all made in the same design.

The large bowl differs from the smaller ones only in that it has a block left in the center to hold the upright shaft and the nut picks. Plate 26.

Because of the cross-lap joint on the spindle work, it will be necessary on the upright piece or shaft to turn to $\frac{7}{8}''$ diameter at the joint, step around the cylinder to make four equal sides, and pare off the wood with a sharp chisel, thus producing the joint part, which is $\frac{5}{8}''$ square. On the cross piece it is possible to start with square stock $\frac{5}{8}''$ and turn on each side of

94

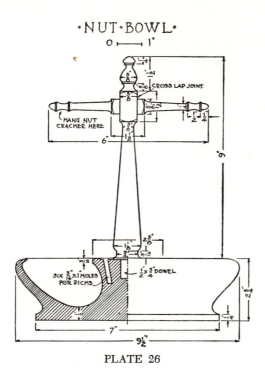

·NUT·BOWL·

PLATE 26

the center. When all sandpapering and turning have been completed, lay out the cross-lap joint, cut to fit snugly, and glue together. The ends will have to be rounded up by hand and the entire project finished at one time when the work has been assembled.

When nutcrackers are used, it is more in keeping to turn down the metal handles to about ¼″ in diameter and then turn wooden handles to be fitted over them, Fig. 81.

Fruit Bowl

This attractive fruit bowl is made of two pieces of wood. Myrtle wood was used for the one shown, Fig. 82, although any good cabinet wood would serve equally well.

The upper or bowl section is turned on a faceplate. Glue the pieces to be turned to scrap stock with paper between. Turn out the inside to conform with a templet; then turn as much of the outside as practical. The remainder is then turned

95

FIGURE 81. This attractive, useful nut set has a large bowl for the nuts and small individual bowls of the same design.

by rechucking the job. Bore the hole for the dowel while the piece is in the lathe.

The base section should be turned on a faceplate. Be careful to make a good flat surface on top for gluing this portion to the bowl part. While it is in the lathe, bore out the hole for the dowel. Plate 27.

When all turning is completed and the pieces are thoroughly sandpapered, glue the two sections together. The small piece of dowel will center the two units while gluing.

FIGURE 82. Attractive and useful fruit bowl made out of myrtle, in two pieces.

·F R U I T · B O W L·

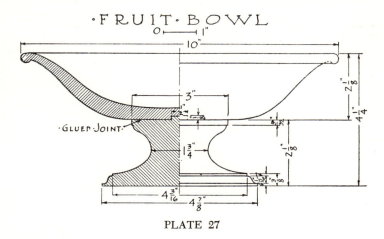

PLATE 27

Finish this project by hand, using lacquer, spar varnish, or hot wax. Plate 28, Fig. 83.

SALAD BOWLS

Have you ever taken a drink of water out of a china or metal cup instead of a glass? Well, it just does not taste re-

97

FIGURE 83. A large highly polished mahogany fruit bowl.

·LARGE·FRUIT·BOWL·

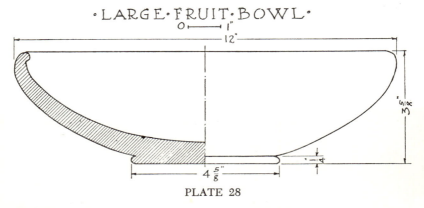

PLATE 28

freshing; it does not satisfy as well as a glass. We know that this is merely our mental attitude, but, nevertheless, we feel a difference. If you have never eaten a green tossed salad out of a wooden bowl, I can tell you, as in the case of water in a glass, you have a real treat in store. Plate 29, Fig. 84.

LARGE·SALAD·BOWL·

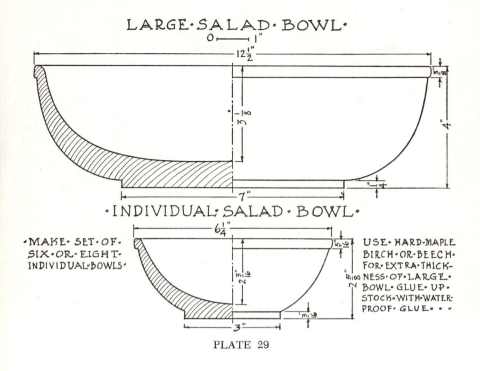

0 ⊢————⊣ 1"

12½"

3⅛"

4"

7"

·INDIVIDUAL·SALAD·BOWL·

6¼"

·MAKE·SET·OF· SIX·OR·EIGHT· INDIVIDUAL·BOWLS·

2 3/16"

3"

USE·HARD·MAPLE BIRCH·OR·BEECH· FOR·EXTRA·THICK- NESS·OF·LARGE· BOWL·GLUE·UP· STOCK·WITH·WATER- PROOF·GLUE···

PLATE 29

FIGURE 84. Make these salad bowls in sets of four or eight, with one large bowl for serving.

FIGURE 85. Elite salad bowl, with metal base, has fork and
spoon made of the same wood.

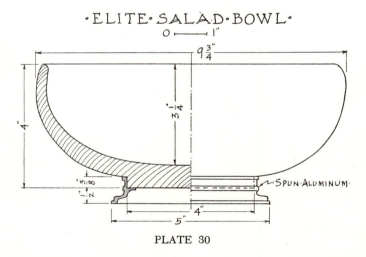

·ELITE·SALAD·BOWL·

PLATE 30

I will show several different designs for salad bowls but all
are turned out in much the same manner. For a salad set, you
should have one large bowl that will contain the salad to be

served, and six or eight smaller individual bowls. For the craftsman who likes to work in metal, I offer one design, and I will also show in my photographic illustation the wooden salad fork and spoon, all trimmed with German silver or aluminum. Plate 30, Fig. 85.

Salad bowls should be made out of maple (use plain, curly, or bird's eye), birch, or myrtle. For instructions on the turning, refer to the preceding discussion of bowls, and for finishing, refer also to that discussion. Fig. 86.

DRAWING SET

If you have occasion to ink in a drawing now and then, you

FIGURE 86. The inside of the bowl is being turned to the required design. A low speed is necessary to reduce vibration.

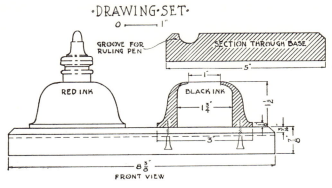

·DRAWING·SET·

GROOVE FOR RULING PEN

SECTION THROUGH BASE

RED INK

BLACK INK

FRONT VIEW

PLATE 31

will appreciate having this drawing set, since it provides a safe container for your bottles of ink and a good place for your ruling pen. The turned wooden holder is slipped over the bottle of ink and screwed to a base piece from the under side so that you will not accidentally knock over the ink. Plate 31.

Use any kind of wood you prefer. This job is first turned

FIGURE 87. This drawing outfit prevents the ink bottles from being knocked over. It has a groove for holding the lettering or ruling pen.

102

from the bottom, is then rechucked so that the face side can be turned. Finish the holder and base piece separately; then assemble. Fig. 87.

Cake and Bread Boards

Aside from the fact that you will no doubt continually use a board of this kind when cutting cake or bread, there will be many other uses the housewife will find for it in her kitchen. Plate 32.

This cake and bread board is easily made. Turn the face surface first; then rechuck and turn the edge and the back. If you are capable of doing wood carving, I suggest that you carve the following inscription around the board, using Gothic letters: "Give us this day our daily bread." Or you perhaps have a favorite inscription you would like to use instead.

You will notice that I show a photograph of a very old bread board that has been in my friend's family for many years; it has the inscription, "Waste not," carved on its border. Fig. 88.

Teapot Stands

If you are interested in metal craft as well as wood turning, I offer these very useful and beautiful teapot stands; they are simple to turn and the metal top lends itself to unlimited art expression. Fig. 89.

Use some choice hardwood like mahogany, rosewood, walnut (either Circassian or American) or any of the darker woods

· CAKE· ₤·BREAD · BOARDS ·

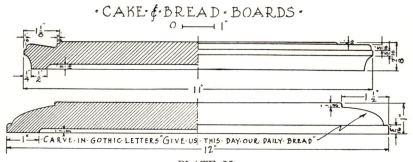

PLATE 32

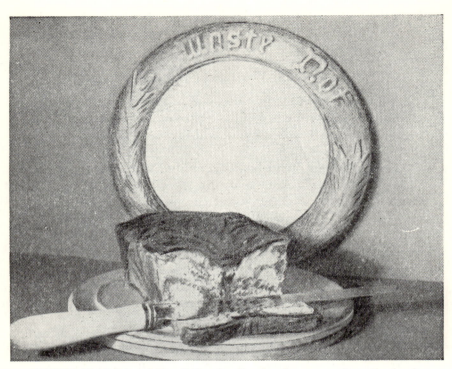

FIGURE 88. Cake and Bread Boards. One has been carved on the border with the words "Waste Not" and a leaf design.

—that is, if you intend using copper for the metal top. If you use German silver and curly or bird's eye maple, a finish in an antique effect will make a very attractive stand. Plate 33.

Turn the under side first; then rechuck and work out the face side and molded edge, Fig. 90.

The metal top is made as follows: Trace your pencil design from the paper onto the metal. Paint all parts, including the back and edge, that are *not* to be etched in acid, with black asphaltic paint. When it is dry, put in a nitric acid bath of proper strength. When it has been etched deep enough (this will require about five hours or more), the etched out background should be tooled, as well as parts of the design if so needed. This metal top, if of copper, should then be colored by heating and dipping in an oil bath, the highlights gently

FIGURE 89. Teapot stands with tops of etched German silver.
Short stem candlesticks.

·TURNING·A·MOLDED·EDGE·

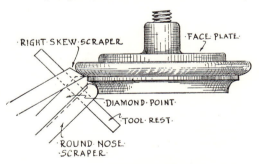

FIGURE 90

rubbed, and then it should be fastened to the wooden stand
with rivets, Fig. 91.

·TEA·POT·STANDS·

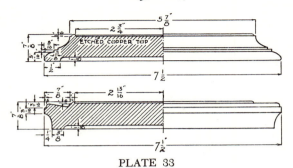

PLATE 33

·TOPS·FOR·TEA POT·STANDS·

·JAPANESE·INFLUENCE·

·GEOMETRIC·PATTERN·

FIGURE 91

106

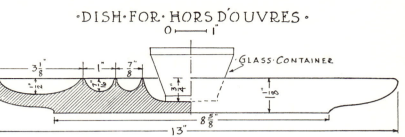

PLATE 34

DISH FOR HORS D'OEUVRES

An attractive and useful article for the craftsman to make, this project can be turned out of any richly figured hardwood such as mahogany, walnut, curly or bird's eye maple, myrtle, etc. It can also be made out of a softer wood and then painted in attractive colors. See Frontispiece.

This is a faceplate job and can be turned all from one side without rechucking. A small glass container (such as tidbits are sold in) should be placed in the center of this dish to hold special sauces for dipping shrimp and the like. Plate 34.

SMOKERS' OUTFIT

This combination ash tray, match box holder, and place for the pipe, cigar, or cigarette will be a welcome addition to any home.

The tray requires only simple faceplate turning. The block for holding the box of matches is easy to make, as also is the piece of bent copper. Plate 35.

HAT STAND AND RING TOSS

These two projects are easy to make. The hat stand can be used by either a man or woman to place a hat on and may be kept in your clothes closet.

The ring toss is part of a simple game the children will enjoy playing. The rings are to be made about 5 or 6 inches in diameter, using rope. The idea of the game is to stand about 8 or 10 feet from the stake and try to toss as many rings as possible on this stake.

107

·SMOKERS' OUTFIT·

0 |—————| 1"

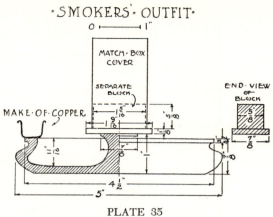

PLATE 35

Use any workable wood and paint this project in a bright color. Plate 36.

STOOLS

Designs for two stools have been given; one is for use in the

·HAT·STAND·&·RING-TOSS·

0 |—————| 1"

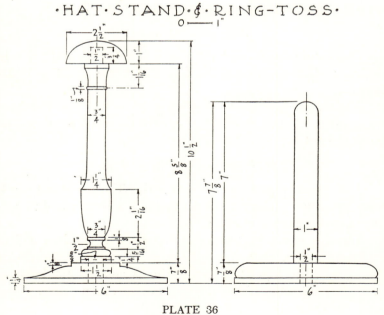

PLATE 36

0 —— 1"

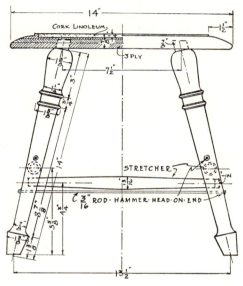

PLATE 37

bathroom; the other is useful equally for either kitchen or shop. The housewife will appreciate a stool in her kitchen when preparing vegetables, etc., and in the shop, a stool is very helpful when doing work at the drill press as well as many other tasks.

The top for the bathroom stool is made with the center portion of cork linoleum, whereas the top of the shop stool is made all of wood but laminated to give extra strength and to keep it from warping. These tops are, of course, faceplate turned and the legs and stretchers are all simply spindle turned. Plate 37.

Metal rods should be used as shown, to prevent the legs from spreading apart; this is of utmost importance. The tops of the four legs should have a saw cut made in them and a wedge in place under pressure when assembling, so as to force the ends apart slightly and thereby assure a premanent tight fit.

Use maple, beech, or birch throughout and assemble the entire stool in one operation. The bathroom stool should be

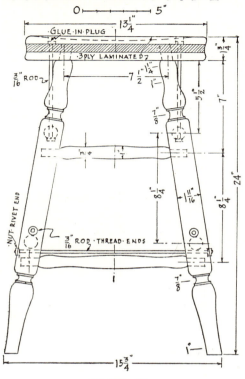

PLATE 38

finished with paint and enamel, colored to your choice; and the shop stool can be finished by applying a liberal coat of boiled linseed oil, followed, when dry, with three thin coats of shellac, varnish, or clear lacquer. The bottoms of the legs must be sawed off by hand so that the stool will rest correctly on the floor. Plate 38, Fig. 92.

THE NAPKIN RING

Napkin rings that are made of the right kinds of wood will give many years usage, provided they are handled with some consideration. Any of the hardwoods are good to use, especially some of the rare varieties such as rosewood, ebony, cocobolo, East Indian mahogany, holly, Circassian walnut, etc. Plate 39.

110

FIGURE 92. A sturdily built stool for any shop or kitchen.

Built-up work—that is, gluing together several different kinds of woods—will make a more attractive napkin ring. The utmost care must be exercised in planing up the stock to get each piece absolutely parallel, and if symmetrical design is used, pieces of the same size should be exactly the same thickness, and, of course, the gluing must be good. Again, when

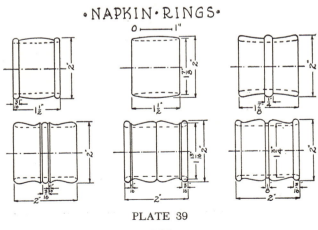

PLATE 39

111

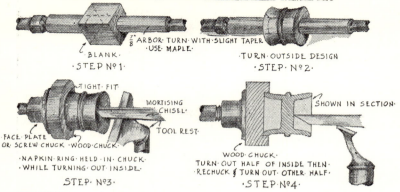

·TURNING·A·NAPKIN·RING·ON·AN·ARBOR·

⅞" ARBOR· TURN· WITH· SLIGHT TAPER
·USE· MAPLE·

·BLANK·
·STEP Nº1·

·TURN· OUTSIDE· DESIGN
·STEP· Nº 2·

·TIGHT· FIT·

MORTISING
CHISEL·

TOOL REST·

FACE· PLATE·
OR· SCREW CHUCK ·WOOD·CHUCK·
·NAPKIN·RING· HELD· IN· CHUCK·
·WHILE TURNING· OUT· INSIDE·
STEP· Nº3·

SHOWN IN SECTION·

WOOD· CHUCK·
TURN· OUT HALF OF INSIDE THEN·
·RECHUCK & TURN OUT· OTHER· HALF·
·STEP· Nº4·

·TURNING· A· NAPKIN·RING· ON·A·SCREW·CHUCK·OR·FACE·PLATE·

·BLANK· FASTENED ·TO·
·A·SCREW· CHUCK·
·STEP · Nº 1·

MORTISING
CHISEL

·STEP· Nº2·
·TURN· TO· CYLINDER· AND·
·TRUE· UP· THE· END·

·STEP· Nº3·
·FACE· UP· END·

FLAT· SCRAPER·

·NOTE: STEP Nº4· TURN· TO· DESIGN·   STEP Nº 5· HOLLOW· OUT· ONE· END· THEN· USE· CHUCK·

FIGURE 93

starting to turn, the exact center must be located; otherwise the design made by the different woods used will come out uneven.

Fig. 93 illustrates the four different steps for the turning of a napkin ring on an arbor. First, Step 1, bore a ⅞" hole all the way through the blank, and at right angles with the stock. For the arbor, turn a separate piece of fairly hard wood between centers, and about 5" long, to fit the ⅞" hole snugly, making a *very* slight taper at the live center end. The blank from which the napkin ring is to be turned is then forced over this arbor. It will make the roughing off easier if the corners of the blank are cut off before placing on the arbor. In Step 2, turn the design, sandpaper, and polish. Now the inside is turned so as to get the proper thickness; to do this, a chuck must first be

112

turned to fit the outside of the napkin ring very tightly. It should be turned with a recess of about ¼". Step 3—now turn the inside of one end a little over half the depth, sandpaper, and polish. Then, Step 4, rechuck and turn, sandpaper, and finish the inside of the other half. It goes without saying that your cut must be a light one and the tools must be kept sharp at all times; otherwise the napkin ring will be forced out of the chuck. To remove the work from the chuck, tap the chuck gently with a mallet; the napkin ring will then spring out.

A second method of turning a napkin ring is on a screw chuck. Bore a hole in the wood, the root diameter of the screw of the chuck, so that, when the chuck is screwed in place, the wood will not split, and yet it must be tight enough to hold the wood firmly. Turn the blank to the design, sandpaper, and polish; then rechuck, turn, and finish as mentioned above.

A third method of turning a napkin ring is to use a bell chuck, Fig. 68. By this method, the blank is first turned between centers with an additional flat part to drive into the chuck. Held by this tight fit, the napkin ring is then turned on the inside as described above. The wood must be long enough so that, after cutting off the napkin ring, about ¾" will remain for rechucking, which is done from the inside instead of the outside as with the other two methods.

The greatest care must be taken to turn the chuck to fit the inside of the ring tight enough so that it will take hold and yet not be a hair's breadth too large; otherwise the napkin ring will be split apart. This method is not recommended by the author, as too often a napkin ring is ruined by splitting and also it takes about 50% more choice wood, whereas, in the other cases, any common wood or scrap wood can be used for the chuck, and if made out of fairly thick stock the same chuck can be used over again for various other projects.

Clock Casing

The clock casing here shown can either be made out of one solid block or built up of segments. The latter method is, of course, best, but more difficult.

After building up the segments to the proper height, turn

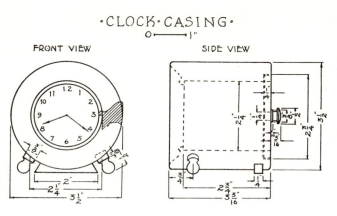

FRONT VIEW   SIDE VIEW

PLATE 40

the cylinder to 3½″ in diameter, hollow out the inside, cut the rabbet for the door, sandpaper, and finish. Now rechuck and turn the molded design on the front. The cover is turned first on the face and then rechucked, after which the knob and two legs are turned between centers.

The cover is hung with a small brass hinge and the knob is glued in place. Bore the hole for the knob on the door with a Foerstner bit, and bore the holes for the legs on the clock case with an auger bit.

When the project is turned from a solid piece of wood, the grain should run with the length; in other words, the face will show end grain.

On account of shrinkage when using a solid piece, it is necessary to make the inside diameter a little large, so that, when the wood contracts, it does not bind around the clock and hold it fast. There is also danger of checking, should the wood shrink considerably. Plate 40.

Tray and Frame Moldings

The method of turning a picture frame, Plate 41, is quite the same as for a napkin ring. In most cases, the screw chuck method will be found to work satisfactorily, although it is often advisable to glue the wood from which the frame is to be made to a piece of scrap wood, with heavy paper between. Turn the

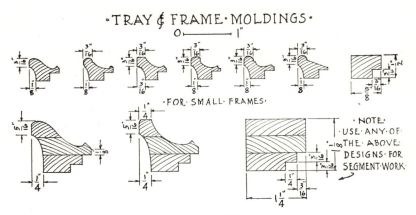

·FOR· SMALL· FRAMES·

·NOTE·
·USE·ANY·OF·
·THE· ABOVE·
·DESIGNS· FOR·
·SEGMENT·WORK·

PLATE 41

front side of the frame; then remove from the chuck and, using the same scrap stock, rechuck for cutting the rabbet, Fig. 94. Large frames are first built up of segments. (See Serving Tray, page 140.)

Turned Oval Picture Frame

Satisfactory oval picture frames can be turned on the lathe by using the two circle method. That is, two separate circular frames are turned, with different diameters, and then two segments are cut from each circular frame. These four segments are then joined together forming the oval.

The success of your oval or elliptical frame depends on two things: First, only certain proportions of the major and minor

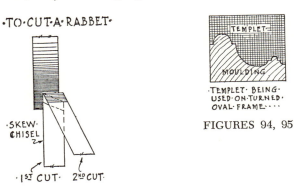

·TO·CUT·A·RABBET·

·SKEW·
CHISEL·

·1ST CUT· 2ND CUT·

TEMPLET

MOULDING

·TEMPLET· BEING·
USED· ON·TURNED·
OVAL· FRAME·····

FIGURES 94, 95

115

axes will work well and therefore should be used; secondly, the large and small circles must be turned with exactly the same molded edge. This last item is accomplished by working from a templet, Fig. 95. Good proportions for the ellipse are, major axis 8″, minor axis 6″; major axis 12″, minor axis 9″, etc., or, in other words, the minor axis is 25% less than the major.

Plate 42 gives the step by step method of procedure; only a few additional directions will be necessary. A quick accurate way of dividing a given space into any number of equal parts is as follows: In this particular case, we want three equal parts, so any number that is a multiple of three, such as 15, will work. This multiple is governed by the measurement of

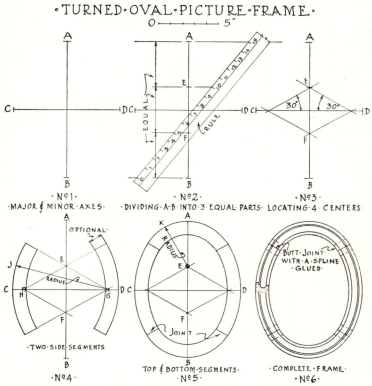

·TURNED·OVAL·PICTURE·FRAME·

STEPS·TAKEN·FOR·LAYING·OUT·AN·OVAL·BY·THE·APPROXIMATE·FOUR CENTER·METHOD··TWO·CIRCLES·TURNED·FROM·WHICH·SEGMENTS·ARE·CUT·

PLATE 42

116

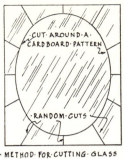

· METHOD· FOR· CUTTING· GLASS ·
· OVAL· IN· SHAPE·

FIGURE 96

the space to be divided. It must always be greater. As shown (Step 2), place zero of the rule on the bottom line; then move the rule around until 15 strikes the upper line; put marks at 5 and 10, thereby making the desired divisions.

The radius of the larger circular frame you turn should be equal to J-G, Step 4. The radius of the smaller circular frame should be equal to K-E, Step 5.

After turning the molded edge on the face side, rechuck so that the rabbet can be cut; do this on both large and small frames. Cut two segments as shown from each frame, working by superimposing on a full size layout; this must be done very carefully. On a circular saw, groove out for the spline. Glue on temporary ears for a grip when gluing.

To cut a piece of glass oval in shape, first cut out a heavy piece of cardboard a little less than the desired size of the glass needed, to allow for the thickness of the glass cutter, Fig. 96. Place the glass on something flat and soft, like a piece of old carpet; score a line around the cardboard form just made; then score tangent lines as shown. Turn the glass bottom side up and place on the piece of carpet; tap around oval gently with the end of the glass cutter.

BOXES

There are two general types of boxes to consider: Those having the cover fitting on the inside, Plate 43 (center), and those having the cover fitting on the outside, Plate 44. Most

117

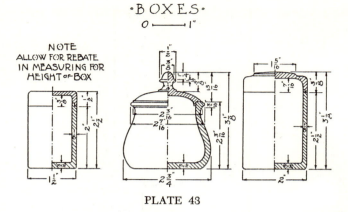

PLATE 43

boxes are the latter type. There is, however, little difference in the turning.

All small boxes should be turned standing on end grain. A

·GIRL'S·DRESSER·SET·

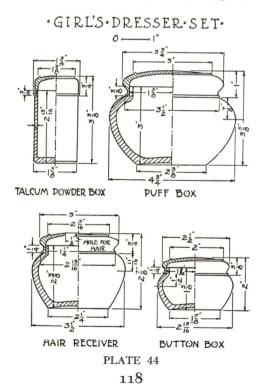

TALCUM POWDER BOX   PUFF BOX

HAIR RECEIVER   BUTTON BOX

PLATE 44

118

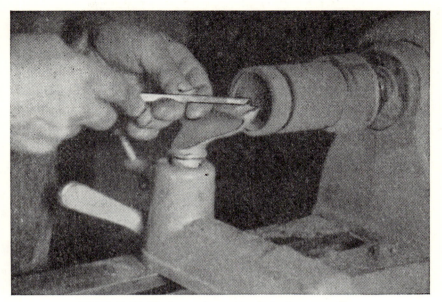

FIGURE 97. Work out the inside of the box cover first.

screw chuck is good to use. Rough off the blank to approxi-
mately the largest diameter. Turn up the end. Now hollow out
the inside of the cover, Fig. 97, Step 1, to conform to a templet
and also turn as much of the top or outside of this cover as
conveniently can be handled. Sandpaper and polish. Cut this
cover section free and remove from the lathe. If the cover fits
from the outside, then cut the collar part of the box on the
remaining portion of a blank; this must be a snug fit, since it
is used for rechucking the cover, Fig. 98. Rechuck the cover
and complete the turning, sandpapering and polishing, Fig. 99.
Remove the cover and proceed to hollow out the inside of the
box to fit the templet (see Bowls). Now sandpaper thoroughly.
Turn the outside to conform with the design; then *slightly* ease
up the collar so that the cover can be removed freely. Thoroughly sandpaper and finish the box portion. Cut the waste
wood away at the bottom to about ½″ in diameter and *slightly*
concave. Saw the box free with a hand saw, clean up with a
sloyd knife; then finish off with felt (see Bowls).

When the cover fits on the inside, great care must be taken

FIGURE 98. The cover is rechucked on the collar part of the box.

when sandpapering the inside of the box portion, not to drag the paper over the top; otherwise the cover will fit too free.

When getting out stock for a box, allow at least ¼″ between the cover and box proper, in order that there will be room for cutting the cover off.

Boxes of large dimensions must be built up of segments.

To remove a chuck or faceplate, use two wrenches as shown in Fig. 100.

GIRL'S DRESSER SET

Here is an attractive set of four boxes for a girl's dresser, all having the same general design but differing in size.

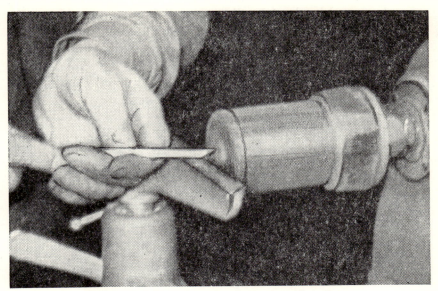

FIGURE 99. The top of the cover is turned to design, sandpapered, and polished.

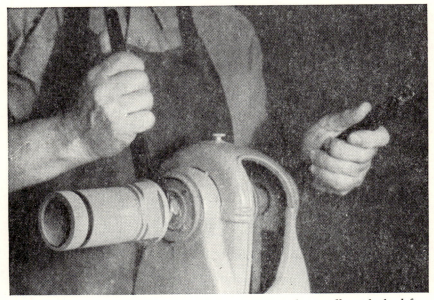

FIGURE 100. Use two wrenches as shown, holding the spindle with the left hand while loosening the screw chuck or faceplate with the right hand.

Any good hardwood will serve well for this project. It will be wise to select some richly figured stock. Curly maple, myrtle, cocobolo, rosewood, and mahogany are all fine woods to use.

For the method of turning, follow the general instructions for boxes given in the preceding discussion. Plate 44.

Chapter Ten

COMBINATION TURNING

Candlesticks, Lamp Standards, Etc.

PROJECTS having both a shaft and base come under this heading and are all turned in much the same manner.

Candlesticks of all kinds will always be popular. Several different designs are here given, for high, low, and medium height candlesticks. The short stem ones are best for use on the dinner table, since they do not obstruct too much of the view of persons seated across the table; of course, they can be used to advantage in many other places, also. Plates 44, 45. Where a touch of dignity and solemnity is required, use the tall designs.

In order to make it easier for the craftsman to follow the instructions, I will use Plate 47 for my project.

The base

Cut a piece of stock 1⅛″ x 5¼″ x 5¼″. Screw this piece to a faceplate, using short screws and keeping them near the out-

·LOW·CANDLESTICKS·

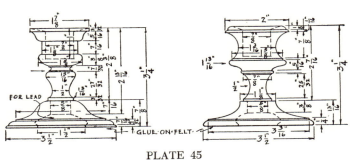

PLATE 45

SHORT STEM CANDLESTICKS

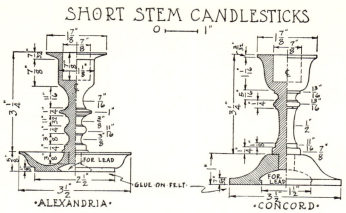

·ALEXANDRIA·   ·CONCORD·

PLATE 46

· SALEM · CANDLESTICK ·

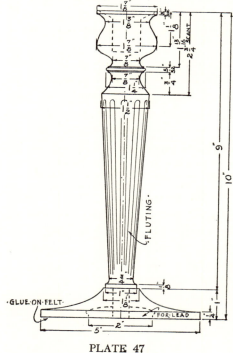

·FLUTING·

·GLUE·ON·FELT·

PLATE 47

124

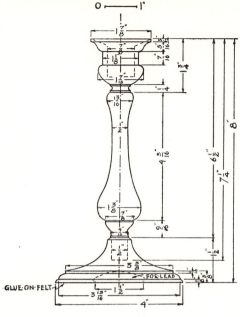

PLATE 48

side edge of the stock so that no holes will remain when the work has been completed. Plates 46, 47, 48.

The base is made in the following manner: Using a mortising chisel, true up the stock on the edge to the largest possible diameter. Now, using the point of the skew chisel held flat, cut this edge to the 5" diameter. With a 1" flat scraper, true up the surface to a trifle over 1" thick. Again, using the mortising chisel (on edge), cut the opening for the lead. Note that the under side of the base is turned first. With a round-nose scraper, shape out this recess for the lead as indicated on the drawing. Sandpaper and polish the work at this stage.

Now remove the wood from the faceplate and rechuck. The recess for the rechucking in this case should be ¼" deep, which is the height of the edge. Using a power auger bit, Foerstner, center bit, or metal drill, bore the ½" hole. Never use an auger bit for lathe boring, as the spur will pull the bit

125

·OLD·LYNN·CANDLESTICK·

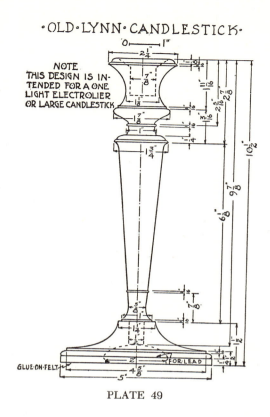

NOTE
THIS DESIGN IS IN-
TENDED FOR A ONE
LIGHT ELECTROLIER
OR LARGE CANDLESTICK

GLUE·ON·FELT

PLATE 49

into the work too fast and may cause an accident. This, however, can be adjusted. (See lathe boring, Chapter Nine.)

When using a Foerstner bit, it will be necessary to cut a
little way down with a $\frac{1}{8}''$ chisel so that the bit will find its
own center. (Foerstner bits have no spur for centering.)

Now shape the face of the base piece to the design and
sandpaper thoroughly. If the job is to be finished in the lathe,
the edge must be polished before rechucking and the remainder polished while in the chuck. Be careful not to get any
oil into the hole; otherwise the glue will not adhere when the
candlestick is assembled.

The shaft

The rough stock to be used should be 2″ x 2″ x 10½″. To

126

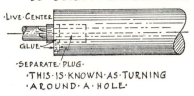

·LIVE·CENTER·

GLUE

·SEPARATE·PLUG·
·THIS·IS·KNOWN·AS·TURNING
·AROUND·A·HOLE·

FIGURE 101

make sure of having a hole in the center (on the top of the shaft), bore a $\frac{7}{8}''$ hole first, and then turn around this hole. In order for you to do this, the hole should be $1\frac{3}{8}''$ deep to allow for cutting off the end later. Now turn a plug between centers to fit this hole and glue it in place as indicated, Fig. 101.

After the glue has set, turn the shaft to design, sandpaper, and polish; then fit the dowel end to the hole in the base. When all polishing is completed, cut the live center end to the length, which will also cut the plug free. It can then be easily removed. It must be noted that the cut on the end is to have a slight bevel to receive the brass fitting that holds the candle.

These fittings can be purchased in most large hardware and department stores.

Place the two parts of the candlestick together (no glue), place the bottom side up, and pour molten lead into the base to come just flush. Cool immediately with a blower or electric fan to prevent the heat of the molten lead from blistering the finish. A small quantity of mercury added to the lead will help prevent blistering of the finish. The mercury gives a lower melting point to this combination. Without the lead in the base, the candlestick would easily tip over.

When the lead has cooled off, glue the base and shaft together. Finish the bottom off by gluing a piece of felt to it.

LAMP STANDARD

When making a lamp standard, regardless of its style, the first concern is to get a hole through the shaft for the wiring. The simpliest way is to cut a groove $\frac{3}{16}''$ deep and $\frac{3}{8}''$ wide on two pieces; then glue these pieces together. Great care must be taken not to spread too much glue on the wood; otherwise,

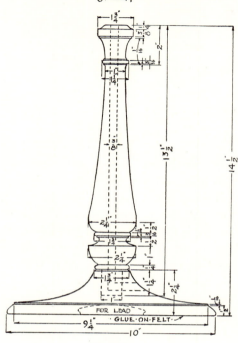

PLATE 50

when it is clamped together, the surplus glue that oozes out will cause trouble later by clogging up the grooves intended for the wiring. Plate 50.

The working out of the remaining portion of the problem is much the same as that of a candlestick; the only difference will be for long shafts. In the case of a long shaft, a steady rest is used. Fig. 117, Plate 51.

For the craftsman who enjoys carving in wood, I offer the classic lamp standard with a fluted shaft and a richly carved base. The acanthus leaf design here shown lends itself well to such a project. The shaft is fluted while held between centers, in the lathe. Always allow a little extra stock for doing the carving. Circassian walnut was used on this project and, when finished in hot wax, it gives a very rich appearance, Fig. 102

128

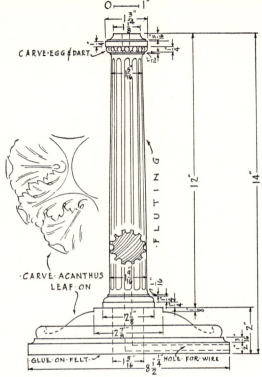

·CLASSIC·LAMP·STANDARD·

CARVE·EGG & DART

FLUTING

CARVE·ACANTHUS
LEAF·ON

GLUE·ON·FELT

HOLE·FOR·WIRE

PLATE 51

BONBON DISHES

Turned bonbon dishes are most attractive, especially when made in many of the richly figured woods, such as curly maple, bird's eye maple, myrtle, cocobolo, rosewood, Circassian walnut, mahogany, etc.

Two designs have been given for these turned dishes, which are to be used for bonbons, chocolates, small cakes, and crackers. One, known as the low style, which is very easy to turn, is deep enough to hold a large quantity of these tidbits. This bowl or dish is made in one piece. The bottom should be turned with a recess to receive lead for weighting. Plate 52.

The second dish is more difficult to turn, as it is made up

129

FIGURE 102. Attractive lamp standard made of Circassian walnut, turned and carved.

of three separate units; this, of course, was done to give the needed strength to the slender shaft part. The dish unit should be turned to design by using a templet. Turn as much of the outside form as possible; then it must be rechucked in order to true up the bottom surface and to cut out to fit the dowel end of the shaft. A simpler but not so accurate a method would be to bore out this hole with a Foerstner bit. The base of this dish is turned on the bottom side first, then rechucked. The shaft section is done with simple spindle turning. Care must be exercised to obtain a good fit at both dowel ends.

It is best to finish this project by hand, after the dish has

BON-BON DISHES

0 —— 1"

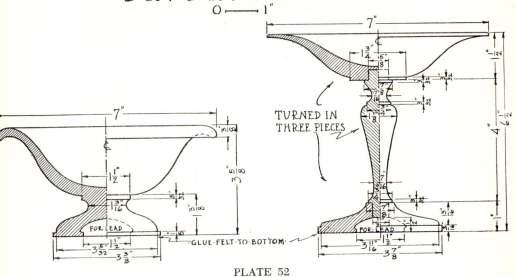

TURNED IN
THREE PIECES

FOR LEAD

GLUE FELT TO BOTTOM

PLATE 52

·UTILITY·FLOWER·HOLDERS·

0 —— 1"

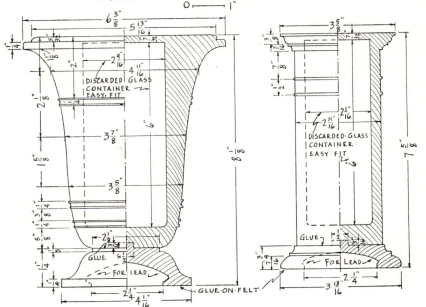

DISCARDED
CONTAINER
EASY·FIT

DISCARDED·GLASS
CONTAINER
EASY·FIT

GLUE

FOR LEAD

GLUE·ON·FELT

FOR LEAD

PLATE 53

131

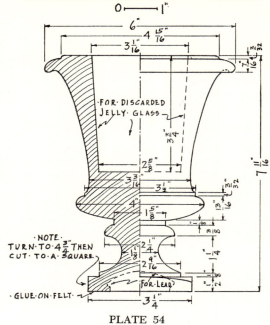

PLATE 54

been glued together. A lacquer job will wear best and be the easiest to keep in good condition.

UTILITY FLOWER HOLDERS

The name "utility" was chosen for this project since these flower holders were designed to utilize discarded glass containers of a variety of sizes, such as the housewife gets when she purchases olives, pickles, mayonnaise, etc. Here is an excellent opportunity for the craftsman to put to good use articles that otherwise are thrown away.

Select your glass container; then, if necessary, slightly change the measurements given to meet your individual requirements. Plate 53.

These holders can be turned by two methods: The simpler way is to bore or turn out the hole to receive the glass container. Plug this hole on the end and then turn between centers. Finish while in the lathe and finally remove the plug. The

132

second method is to do all turning on a small faceplate. Either way will prove satisfactory. Plate 54.

FLOWER HOLDER

Here is a useful project of pleasing design, easy to turn.

Bore out the hole to receive the glass container on either a drill press or in your lathe. Make this hole large enough so that the container can easily be removed; avoid a tight fit.

After the hole has been bored, turn a plug between centers to fit; glue this in place.

The job is then turned around this plugged hole much the same as explained for the candlesticks. Plate 55.

SHIP'S WHEEL MIRROR

Although used as a mirror, this ship's wheel makes an

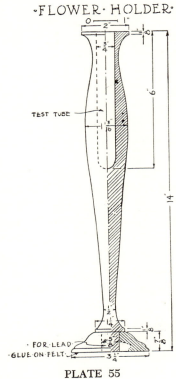

·FLOWER· HOLDER·

PLATE 55

133

SHIP'S WHEEL MIRROR

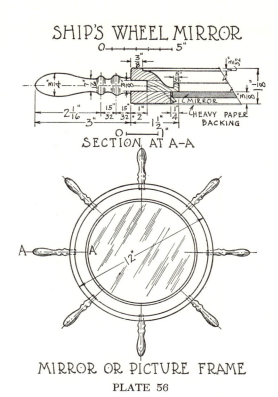

SECTION AT A-A

MIRROR OR PICTURE FRAME

PLATE 56

equally good picture frame, especially if you are nautically inclined.

The handles require only simple spindle turning. Use 1" square stock, about 4½" long. The dowel ends must be turned to fit snugly into a ⅜" hole that has been bored with an auger bit and brace. The handles should be finished in the lathe. Plate 56.

The frame part is built up of segments, eight to each course, as shown on the drawing. Turn up the face molding first; then rechuck and turn out the rabbet, Fig. 94. Refer to the following pages, 135, 136, 137, on segment work.

Great care must be exercised when boring the holes in the frame to receive the handles, so that these holes will radiate to the center. When the mirror or picture, as the case may be, has been put into place, the back of the frame should be neatly sealed by gluing heavy paper over it. Wet the paper, all but the edge which is to be glued, so that, when the paper dries out and shrinks, the back will stretch out tight and smooth.

Any choice wood of richly figured grain will work nicely for this project. Since the job is made up of segments, only small pieces will be required.

Segment Work

In order to turn large disk shaped objects, so that there will be practically no warping, changing of shape, and, at the same time, no sacrifice of strength, it will be necessary to employ the segment type of construction.

The theory of segment work is similar to that of a butt spliced joint, used in carpentry, that has a cleat fastened on each side. By "breaking the joints," as it is called, all parts are equal in strength and, when properly glued together, with the grain of each segment running the long way, the work is stronger than a solid piece. As will be shown, an odd number of courses always proves most efficient.

There can be no set rule as to the number of segments for each course; small circles are usually made of three or six segments; for large diameters, as many as twelve are used.

In starting segment work, it will first be necessary to true up a piece of white pine, or other good wood, to the desired diameter. This, of course, is done on a faceplate and must be turned. It is best first to glue a piece of heavy paper to this piece and then lay off the segments with a pencil on this paper surface. On this foundation piece, the segments are glued and held in place until all turning and finishing have been completed. For six segments, step the radius around the circumference six times and join these points with lines, radiating to the center. The lines just drawn will indicate the joints for the first, third, and fifth courses, and so on, according to the number of courses used.

Divide each space in half, and again draw lines radiating to the center so as to indicate the joints for the second, fourth, and sixth courses, etc., Fig. 103.

135

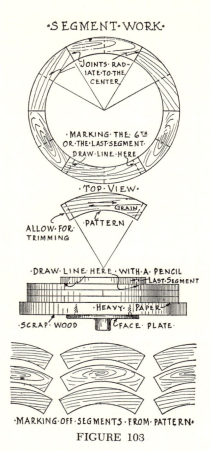

·SEGMENT·WORK·

JOINTS·RAD-
IATE·TO·THE
CENTER

·MARKING·THE·6TH·
OR·THE·LAST·SEGMENT·
DRAW·LINE·HERE

·TOP·VIEW·

GRAIN

ALLOW·FOR·
TRIMMING

·PATTERN·

·DRAW·LINE·HERE·WITH·A·PENCIL
LAST·SEGMENT

·HEAVY·⅛·PAPER·

·SCRAP·WOOD
·FACE·PLATE·

·MARKING·OFF·SEGMENTS·FROM·PATTERN·

FIGURE 103

In order to hold the work while building up the various courses of segments, take a piece of 2″ square stock and turn one end to fit into the threaded part of the faceplate; the square end is clamped in the vise as shown, Fig. 104. The greatest care must be exercised to clamp each segment absolutely flat, making a tight joint all around. To do this, the shoulder spindle of the hand screw is tightened first, throwing the jaws *slightly* out of parallel. Then the last turn or two on the end spindle will bring the jaws to the correct position and glue will ooze out, as it should, all around the segment.

The segments are cut out by first making a cardboard or thin wooden pattern the shape and the outline size of one seg-

FIGURE 104. A good way to support the job while building up the
various courses of segments.

ment; this, of course, should be made a little oversize to allow
for trimming the joint at both ends and turning to the exact
size when all segments have been glued in place.

Cut the segments for the entire job on a band saw; then
glue the first segment in place after trimming the ends to
match the exact joint. A disk sander is ideal for trimming the

137

joint. Fit the second segment in place; then glue the one end joint of the segment already in place and also the flat portion of this segment. Continue with the others, except for the last segment. This will need some special attention when fitting to the others. Fig. 103 illustrates the best method for getting a tight fit at both ends.

Use a good quality hot glue and allow at least four hours for the glue to set and harden before attempting any turning. Working on slow speed, face up the first course of segments to the desired thickness and, at the same time, clean up the outside and inside diameters just a little. Now mark out the second course and continue all the courses as with the first one. When all the courses have been glued in place, do all necessary turning and finishing.

To remove this turned segment band from the foundation piece, split the paper joint apart by placing a broad flat chisel in the glued joint; tap gently in several places around the circle, or until the paper has separated.

SEWING SET

Like some of the other projects, the sewing set or stand is simply a combination of several preceding problems. The base is turned in the same manner as that of the candlesticks. The flat disk is made from a piece of ⅜″ plywood turned on edge,

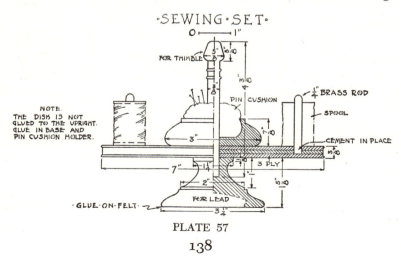

·SEWING·SET·

PLATE 57

138

FIGURE 105. This sewing outfit can revolve, and has a handy pin cushion in the center and a place for the thimble.

and the pin cushion holder is nothing more than a bowl with a hole in the center, which in turning fits snugly around the spool spindle.

In gluing this project, Plate 57, together, be sure *not* to glue the flat disk, as it would then be impossible to make it revolve. The brass dowels are ¼″ in diameter and set in place with a good cement. The pin cushion holder is made with a hole through the center.

Either use a wood to harmonize with your sewing cabinet, etc., or use a wood to be in complete contrast with such articles so as to make the sewing set outstanding. Fig. 105.

Cheese-and-Crackers Dish

This cheese-and-crackers dish is made up of three separate units—the base, the dish and the cup.

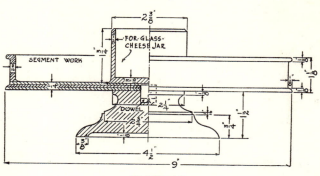

·CHEESE & CRACKER·DISH·

PLATE 58

The base is turned like the base part of a candlestick. The dish can be made by starting with a piece of ¼″ laminated stock, or it can be made with the top layer having segments all coming to a point. This last method will greatly enhance the project. The outside rim of the dish is segment work. The cup portion is a simple bit of faceplate or screw chuck turning.

This project should be assembled first, then finished by hand afterward.

Any good workable cabinet wood will be satisfactory for this article. Plate 58.

SERVING TRAY

A serving tray is nothing more than a large picture frame, with two rabbets on the back. Because of the large size, it will be necessary to build this job up with segments.

Refer to the chapter on segment work for the general instructions. When rechucking, do this job from the inside of the frame, to avoid marring the finish. See Plate 41.

The first rabbet will hold the glass and designed material for the bottom of the tray. (The latter is stretched over cardboard.) The second rabbet is for the wooden bottom, which is screwed in place, flush with the bottom of the molding. The handles are fitted to come flush and are firmly fastened with screws from the under side of the molding. The entire bottom

140

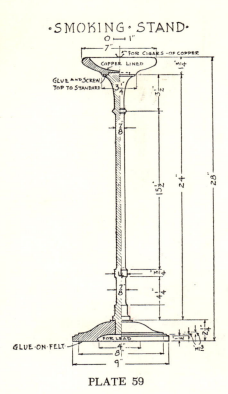

PLATE 59

is then covered with felt, previously stretched over cardboard, with the edges glued on the reverse side. Tack this felt covered cardboard to the tray molding with 2 oz. gimp tacks. Screw four small rubber bumpers in place, completing the job.

By putting the tray together in this manner, should the glass break, it is a simple matter to take out the necessary screws and lift the tacks without destroying any of the tray.

Any richly figured cabinet wood will do well for this project. As little pieces only are required, this will be a good opportunity to use odds and ends of fine wood you may have on hand. Plate 41, Fig. 104.

CROQUET SET

Although an old game, croquet is still very popular and to play it well requires more than ordinary skill.

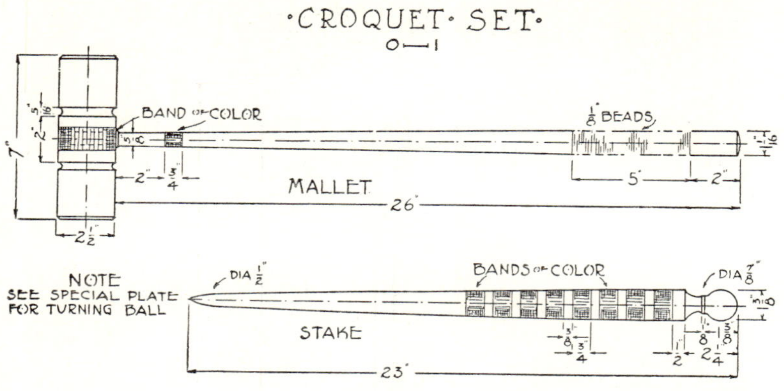

·CROQUET· SET·

O—I

BAND of COLOR | BEADS

MALLET 26″ 2″ ¾ 5″ 2″

NOTE
SEE SPECIAL PLATE
FOR TURNING BALL

DIA ½″ BANDS of COLOR DIA ⅞″

STAKE 23′

PLATE 60

Cheap croquet sets are usually made of hard maple; for a better job, however, use lignum vitae for the balls and heads of the mallets and hickory or ash for the handles. Maple is satisfactory for the stakes. Plate 60.

The mallet is turned much the same as a joiner's mallet, except that a steady-rest, Fig. 117, is required when turning the long slender handles. To use the steady-rest, place the square stock in the lathe, turn a small section in the center to the largest possible diameter; put the steady-rest in place; then turn both halves of the handle to design, remove the rest, and, while supporting the work with the left hand, turn down this center portion with the right hand, to conform with the rest of the handle. Sandpaper smooth. Use a fairly slow speed for all this long thin turning. Fig. 106.

The turning of the ball is accomplished by employing our knowledge of geometry. As we indefinitely increase the number of sides of a polygon, we approach a circle for a limit. First turn a cylinder of 3½″ in diameter; then locate the center and measure 1¾″ on each side of this line, cut to this length (a cross section through the axis forms a perfect square), Fig. 107. We intend, as it were, to inscribe an imaginary circle in this square. Our next step will be to cut so as to make the section into an octagon. Having reached this point, we now cut so as to make the section a 16 sided figure, and so on until we

142

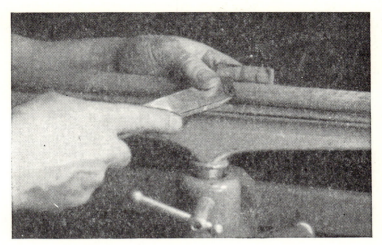

FIGURE 106. Making the final cut with the skew chisel held in the right hand and further supported by the thumb of the left hand. A pad of heavy felt or a piece of leather is used to prevent burning the left hand.

attain 64 sides. At this point, the figure is almost round. Trim off the corners and sandpaper thoroughly.

It is advisable to lay out the circle of 3½″ on paper; then each time construct a square, octagon, etc., inside the circle. From this layout, you can get the exact measurements. The ones given on the drawing are approximate.

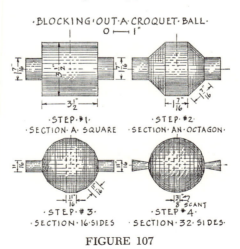

FIGURE 107

143

FIGURE 108. An improvised sanding disk made by simply tacking a piece of sandpaper over a piece of faceplate stock. It is used here to sand the end of a croquet mallet head.

It will be observed that we do not cut the waste wood at either end below ⅜″, leaving the final cutting to be done by hand with a saw and sharp knife, and cleaned up with a file

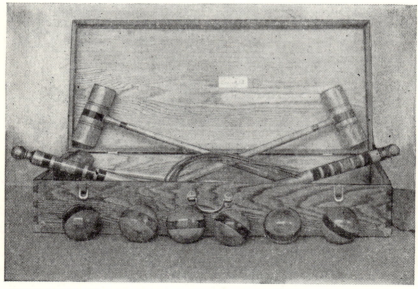

FIGURE 109. This croquet set is not only an excellent wood turning project but an old favorite among games.

and sandpaper. On account of shrinkage in one direction only (across the grain), it will be advisable to cut the end grain of the ball about $\frac{1}{32}''$ less in diameter than the width. When the wood dries out thoroughly, the ball will be as round as it is possible to turn one. Great care must be exercised to mark off the work accurately and then to cut each time to the line. Each flat surface cut is a tangent to the imaginary sphere.

Before cleaning off the center line, cut a line $\frac{3}{8}''$ on each side of it with the toe of a skew chisel. This band is needed for a guide in painting the color on the ball. This method is also employed on the stake and head of the mallet for locating color bands, Fig. 109, Plate 60.

After the mallets have been assembled, apply a liberal coat of boiled linseed oil to the balls, stakes, and mallets. Allow several days to dry and then apply a thin coat of white shellac. Paint the color bands where required (using different and brilliant oil colors) and, when this is dry, apply two coats of spar varnish to the entire piece. Fig. 109.

Cape Cod Fence Posts

The old fence posts here shown represent some of the finest examples that could be found on Cape Cod about two decades ago, and are typical of old New England designs. Many of these posts show considerable wear as the results of exposure to the weather for a good number of years; for that reason the detail drawings may vary slightly from the original posts.

Fence posts should be made out of one of the following woods. I will list them in the order of preference. Fig. 110.

Class 1 (over 20 yrs.)	Class 2 (10 to 20 yrs.)	Class 3 (5 to 10 yrs.)
California Redwood	White Oak	Slippery Elm
Black Locust	Swamp White Oak	Black Cherry
Red Cedar	Honey Locust	Chestnut Oak
Tide Water Cypress	White Cedar	Butternut
Red Mulberry	Black Walnut	Larch
Osage Orange		Ironwood
Catalpa		Apple
		Sassafras

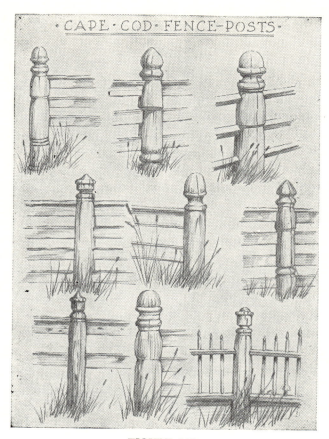

FIGURE 110

To lengthen the durability of woods in Classes 2 and 3, treat these woods by submerging in a five per cent solution of penta-chlorophenol (trade name "Penta"), sold as a wood preservative, for a period of 48 to 72 hours, depending on which class the wood comes under. This soaking is for the 3 foot portion of the post that is set in the ground. Plate 61.

Many of these fine old posts shown here were made of chestnut, which was the farmer's choice at the time I was a boy. The chestnut tree has died off as a result of a blight and now only dead trees can be found, which are of little value for posts.

146

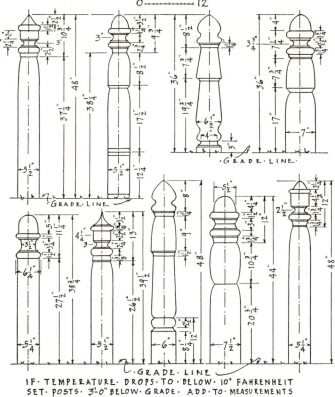

·CAPE·COD·FENCE–POSTS·

IF·TEMPERATURE·DROPS·TO·BELOW·10° FAHRENHEIT
SET· POSTS· 3'-0" BELOW· GRADE· ADD·TO·MEASUREMENTS

PLATE 61

In localities where temperatures drop to below 10° Fahrenheit, the posts should be of sufficient length so that they can be set in the ground 3 feet below the grade to prevent heaving.

TURNED MOLDINGS

There is an unlimited number of designs that could be created for turned moldings. Those shown give quite a good variety and should prove very useful in connection with cabinet work.

The diameter you make the molding will naturally depend upon where it is to be used. This work is done as split turning;

147

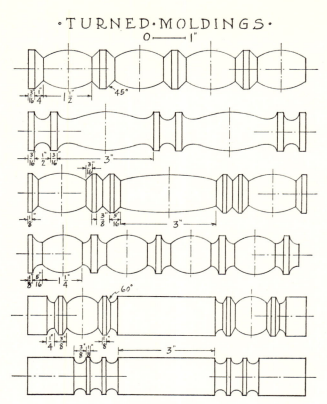

PLATE 62

that is, two halves are glued together with paper between them, then split apart after the turning has been completed.

Very long strips are made up of a series of short pieces. It is best to use a steady-rest because of the small diameters and length. Carving on some of the designs enhances the molding. Turned in one piece, these designs can be used as spindles, stretchers, etc., in furniture and carpentry work. Plate 62.

TEA WAGON WHEEL

The tea wagon wheel presents no new problem except in the making of the hub; this is constructed in the form of two pieces, which, it will be seen, has a decided advantage over a one piece job when assembling.

148

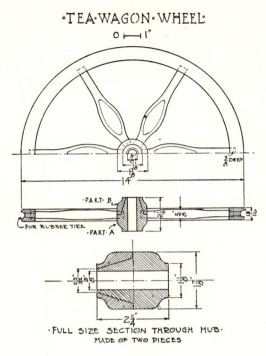

·TEA·WAGON·WHEEL·

·FULL SIZE SECTION THROUGH HUB·
MADE OF TWO PIECES

PLATE 63

The rim is made up of three courses of segments with six segments to each course. Turn this rim as shown on the drawing, and sandpaper smooth. The spokes are turned from 5/8″ flat stock. This will produce the interesting design on both sides. Be careful, when turning the dowel ends, to get a good fit with a 3/8″ hole. Plate 63.

The utmost care must be taken when turning the hub, so that both parts fit perfectly. After this has been done, clamp these two parts together in a vise and bore the six holes to receive the spokes. Make a pencil mark across the joint to assure the same position of both parts when finally assembling. Also bore holes in the rim for the spokes.

Much of the success in making a wheel is in the assembly. For that reason, it will be well to go through the entire set-up for gluing, several times (but, of course, without glue), so that

149

there can be no slip when actually doing the real gluing and no lost time or lost motion, as speed counts when using hot glue.

To assemble, block up the spokes and rim from the under side to come level with the hub; this will bring all spokes in line. The six spokes are each put in place in the rim and one part of the hub (the A part). Now place the B part of the hub in place and, by forcing this down in perfect contact, the entire wheel will stiffen out flat and true. After you are sure of yourself, and with the aid of another pair of hands, to hold parts in place, clamp down the rim; then apply glue to the spokes and holes and finally to the hub and spokes. Force down the hub and clamp this securely. If properly done, the wheel will be strong and run true.

MARBLEHEAD TEA WAGON

Tea wagons will always be popular in our American homes, and rightly so, since they save so many steps when serving refreshments, coffee, or tea in the living room, on the porch, or out on the lawn. The outstanding feature of this tea wagon is the ease with which it can be wheeled in either direction; this has been accomplished by placing the large wheels in the center; then the small wheels simply function like large casters. Plate 64.

The serving tray is an essential part of this project. Use richly figured stock throughout to enhance the beauty of this model. Mahogany, walnut, curly maple, and cherry are all good woods to use.

For instructions about turning the large wheels, refer to the preceding pages on the tea wagon wheel.

SMOKING AND COFFEE TABLE

You will find this smoking and coffee table a very handy and attractive piece of furniture to have. The table is made low so that it will be suitable for both smoking and serving refreshments, coffee, or tea.

The drawers, which open from opposite sides of the table, are quite an unusual feature that is very desirable. Cigarettes or other smoking material should be kept in these drawers.

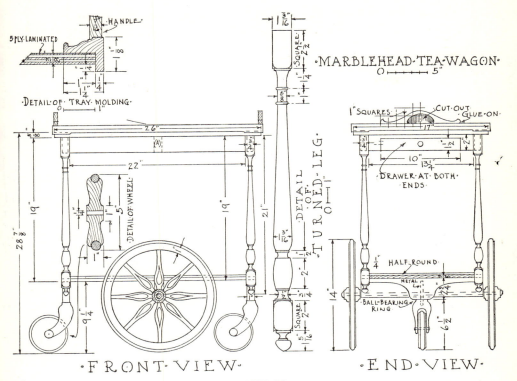

·HANDLE·

5 PLY·LAMINATED

·DETAIL·OF·TRAY·MOLDING·

·MARBLEHEAD·TEA·WAGON·

·DETAIL·OF·TURNED·LEG·

1" SQUARES

·CUT·OUT·
·GLUE·ON·

·DRAWER·AT·BOTH·
ENDS·

·DETAIL·OF·WHEEL·

¼" HALF·ROUND·

METAL
·BALL·BEARING·
RING·

·FRONT·VIEW·

·END·VIEW·

PLATE 64

Great care should be exercised, when turning the legs, not to chip off the sharp square corners at the top and intermediate part of the legs and bottom rails. Plate 65.

The mortise-and-tenon type of construction has been shown, but dowel joints, although not as good, can, of course, be used instead. To assemble, glue up the ends first. Then do the entire table. Be sure to build in the drawer supports when doing the second gluing operation.

The kind of wood you use will depend upon the finish you desire and upon the other furniture in the room which you wish to match.

Mexican mahogany, American black walnut, curly and bird's eye maple and cherry are all good woods to use. Select richly figured stock for all parts. The top will look well made

151

SMOKING AND COFFEE TABLE

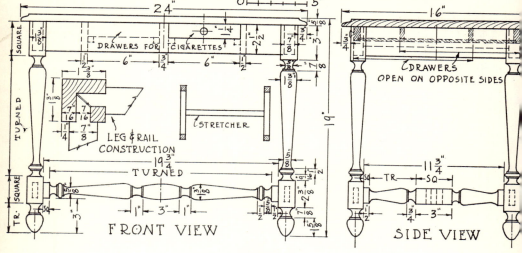

PLATE 65

up of two pieces with a matched effect of the grain at the joint, or run a few lines of inlay or marquetry work in a conventional design.

TRESTLE GATE TABLE

This dainty, beautiful table of Colonial design can be put to many different uses. For example, with one flap down, it serves equally well as a small hall console or an end table, and in the bedroom it may be used as a bedside table.

After turning the legs, cut all mortises and the tenon on one end. When assembling, first glue the feet to the legs (note the through mortise-and-tenon pinned joint). Plate 66.

Allow ample time for the glue to set; then assemble the entire table. Be sure to put the gates in place at the time of assembling the legs, top rail, and turned stretchers.

Allow the tenons, as well as the wooden pins, to project slightly beyond the surface, as shown, to give a genuine hand-made touch, so essential to this model.

Mahogany, walnut, curly maple, or cherry is each an appropriate wood to use.

152

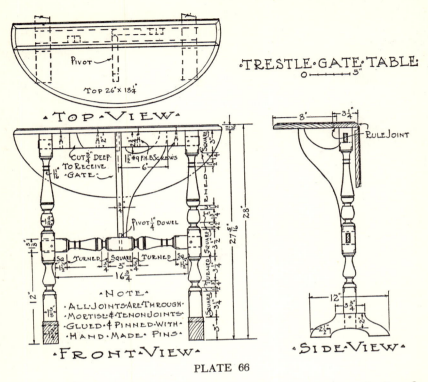

·TRESTLE·GATE·TABLE·

0 ——————— 5"

·TOP·VIEW·

TOP 26" X 18¾"

PIVOT

CUT ¾" DEEP·
·TO·RECEIVE·
·GATE·

1½"#9 F.H.B.SCREWS
6"

PIVOT ¼" DOWEL

Sq. TURNED | SQUARE | TURNED | Sq.
3"

16¾"

·NOTE·
·ALL·JOINTS·ARE·THROUGH·
·MORTISE·&·TENON·JOINTS·
·GLUED·&·PINNED·WITH·
·HAND·MADE·PINS·

·FRONT·VIEW·

·RULE·JOINT·

·SIDE·VIEW·

PLATE 66

Run the molded edge and rule joint on a shaper or by hand, Figs. 111 and 112.

HANDY GATE-LEG TABLE

It is safe to say that no table has become so popular in our American homes of today as the gate-leg table. This is easy to understand, because most people want a table that will collapse into a small space and yet open to a good sized table. An-

·RULE·JOINT·ON·TABLE·TOP·

1"X3" BACK·FLAP·(HINGE)

FIGURE 111

153

FIGURE 112. This trestle gate table can be put to many uses.

FIGURE 113. A fine group of Colonial furniture,
made for the most part on a lathe.

155

other feature which this type table possesses is the fact that the table serves so many different uses. It can be used as an end table, with one flap down, or as a full round table. This particular model is made low so as to serve these uses just mentioned, Fig. 113.

The top can be made with a square hinged joint as shown, or, for a better job, use the rule joint, Fig. 111. When, however, a rule joint is used, allow extra stock. The top can be turned on

HANDY GATE-LEG TABLE

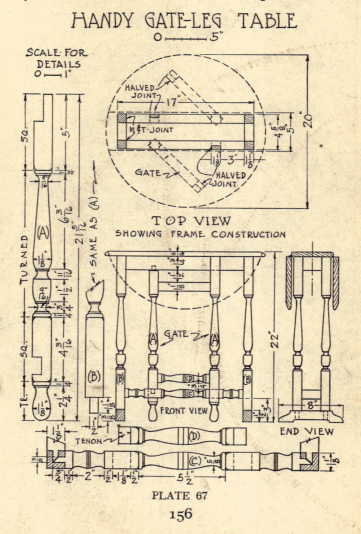

PLATE 67

a lathe, but it is more advisable to cut out the circle on a band saw and then run the molded edge on a shaper or work it out by hand.

The legs and rails are turned in the usual manner; be careful not to chip off the corners of the square portions. After the turning has been completed, cut all joints and make a trial fitting *without* glue to make sure that all parts will fit properly. Plate 67.

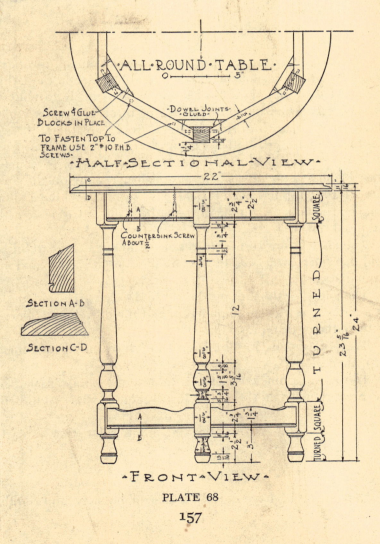

·ALL·ROUND·TABLE·

·HALF·SECTIONAL·VIEW·

SCREW & GLUE BLOCKS IN PLACE

TO FASTEN TOP TO FRAME USE 2"#10 F.H.B. SCREWS·

·DOWEL JOINTS· ·GLUED·

SECTION A-B

SECTION C-D

COUNTERSINK SCREW ABOUT ½

TURNED

TURNED SQUARE

·FRONT·VIEW·

PLATE 68

157

When assembling, glue up the two end sections and the two gates first; then assemble the entire project, fitting the gates in place at this gluing.

Any good cabinet wood will be suitable to use, especially curly maple finished in an antique effect—that is, by lightly rubbing the highlights of the turned portions to add snap and vigor to the table.

Note how this table is used in the group of Colonial furniture, Fig. 113.

ALL-ROUND TABLE

This attractive table, which may be put to many uses, can be made entirely by machinery—the greater part on the lathe.

Select good dry stock for the top. This is likely to hold in shape better when made up of two or three pieces, carefully glued together. To turn the top, use a 10" faceplate and fasten this to the under side with #14 screws. The length will depend upon the thickness of your faceplate. The screws, of course, must be short enough so that they will not show on the face side after the top has been turned. This turning will have to be done on the outside spindle of the lathe, using a tripod or pedestal tool rest, Fig. 2.

The six legs are turned in the usual manner; be careful to hold the sharp corners on the square portions at the top and intermediate part.

The joints for the rails can be cut to the exact size and angle on a circular saw or in a miter box, and the dowel joints bored on the lathe or drill press. Plate 68.

Temporary ears, Fig. 114, must be glued on all rails for a grip when gluing.

The entire framework of this table must be assembled in one operation. To do this job, you will require someone to help you.

Any good cabinet woods are suitable for this project. Fig. 115.

COLONIAL NEST OF TABLES

Nests of tables have never lost their popularity, and rightly

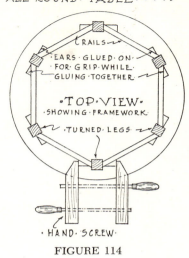

(RAILS
·EARS·GLUED·ON·
·FOR·GRIP·WHILE·
GLUING·TOGETHER·

·TOP·VIEW·
·SHOWING·FRAMEWORK·

·TURNED·LEGS·

·HAND·SCREW·

FIGURE 114

so, for they lend themselves to many uses. They are ideal as an end table and invaluable when serving tea, coffee, or refreshments in the living room. The distinctive thing about them is, of course, that a group of tables, when nested together, takes up no more room than a single table, Fig. 116.

The design here shown is delicate and graceful. The slender legs must be turned by means of a steady-rest, Fig. 117. Get out the stock for these legs a little oversize, but be sure they are straight and true. After the turning has been completed, the square portions can be brought down to the exact size. Plate 69.

Because of the small dimensions of the stock, use dowel construction throughout. Use good dry stock for the top or, better yet, five-ply laminated wood made of richly figured mahogany; walnut, maple, or cherry are also fine woods to use.

The top is glued to the body part, which makes the table rigid. The narrow line of inlay and marquetry work adds much to the charm of these tables.

TILT-TOP TABLE

This tilt-top table, which is a copy of an old Colonial piece,

159

FIGURE 115. This "all-round" table can be made almost entirely on a lathe. An excellent project for both spindle and large faceplate turning.

is different from the commonly known tilt-top type of tables. It is more along the lines of the gate-leg table, but is much

FIGURE 116. The slender, graceful legs of this nest of tables were turned by the aid of a steady-rest.

FIGURE 117. For all slender turning, use a steady-rest; this one is equipped with ball-bearing fittings which greatly reduce friction. Here being used on the Colonial nest of tables.

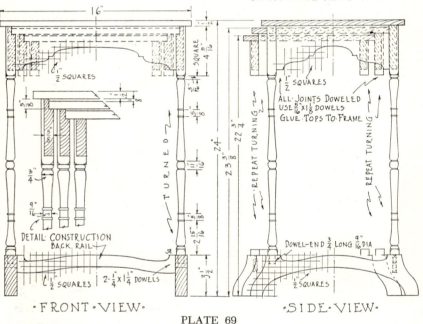

·LINE·OF·INLAY·

MARQUETRY

2¾"

11½"

12"

·TOP·VIEW·

COLONIAL·NEST·OF·TABLES
0 ———— 5"

·NOTE·
THE· SMALLEST· TABLE· HAS· RAILS
ON· ALL· SIDES· FOR· OTHER· TWO
TABLES· NO· RAIL· IN· THE· FRONT
AT· THE· TOP· OR· BOTTOM· · RUN
AN· ⅛· LINE· OF· INLAY· PLACED· ¾"
FROM· EDGE· AND· CENTER· MOTIF
ON· ALL· THREE· TABLE· TOPS

16"

1 ½ SQUARES

5/100

¾"

9/16"

DETAIL· CONSTRUCTION
BACK· RAIL

1 ½ SQUARES | 2·¼ x 1·¼ DOWELS

SQUARE
4 5/16

T U R N E D

24"

22¾"

23⅜"

3½"

·FRONT·VIEW·

1 ½ SQUARES

ALL· JOINTS· DOWELED
USE 5/16 x 1⅝ DOWELS
GLUE· TOPS· TO· FRAME

R E P E A T   T U R N I N G

R E P E A T   T U R N I N G

DOWEL·END ¾ LONG 9/16 DIA

1 ½ SQUARES

·SIDE·VIEW·

PLATE 69

more compact when folded together and has often been called
the "tuck-away table." In this position, the top is placed vertical. Plate 70.

Be careful when turning the legs and stretchers not to chip
off the square corners. The top can be turned on the lathe or
cut on the band saw and then the molded edge run on a shaper.

The pivoting section must be assembled first; then, when

162

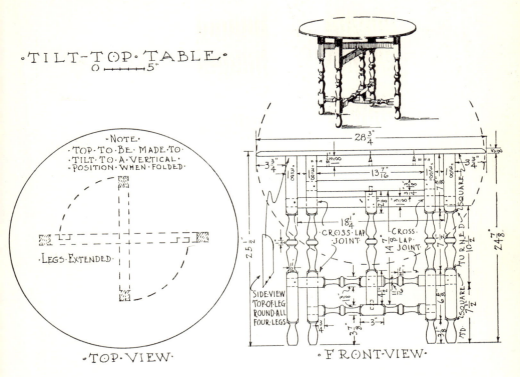

·TILT-TOP·TABLE·
0 ⊢——————⊣ 5"

·NOTE·
·TOP·TO·BE·MADE·TO·
·TILT·TO·A·VERTICAL·
·POSITION·WHEN·FOLDED·

·LEGS·EXTENDED·

·TOP·VIEW·

28 3/4"

13 7/16"

18 1/4"
·CROSS·LAP·
JOINT·

·CROSS·
·LAP·
·JOINT·

25 1/2"

SIDE·VIEW·
TOP·OF·LEG
ROUND·ALL
FOUR·LEGS

·FRONT·VIEW·

PLATE 70

assembling the other part, this first section must be fitted in place.

Use mahogany, walnut, maple, or cherry for this table. When finishing, bring up the highlights of the turned members.

On account of the great width of this table, it is advisable to glue together several pieces instead of using wide stock. If the top is to be turned on a lathe, first true up the bottom surface by hand; then fasten this to a large faceplate. Allow at least $3/16''$ of extra thickness for facing up the top surface. Be sure to use short enough screws so that they will not show on the finished surface.

The most rapid way, however, is to cut the top out accurately on a band saw and then run the edge on a shaper.

163

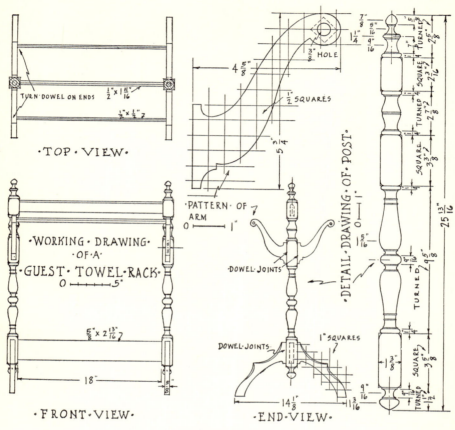

·TOP·VIEW·

·WORKING·DRAWING·
·OF·A·
·GUEST·TOWEL·RACK·
0 ⊢———┤ 5"

·FRONT·VIEW·

·PATTERN·OF·
ARM
0 ⊢———┤ 1"

·DETAIL·DRAWING·OF·POST·
0 ⊢———┤ 1"

·END·VIEW·

PLATE 71

GUEST TOWEL RACK

Although primarily intended for the guest room, this project is welcome anywhere for the fairly large family, since it provides a suitable place to hang wet towels and washcloths.

This is a copy of a fine old Colonial piece. The slender legs need to be turned by using a steady-rest, Fig. 117. Use dowel construction throughout. Plate 71, Fig. 118.

FIGURE 118. This guest towel rack is a copy of an old Colonial piece.

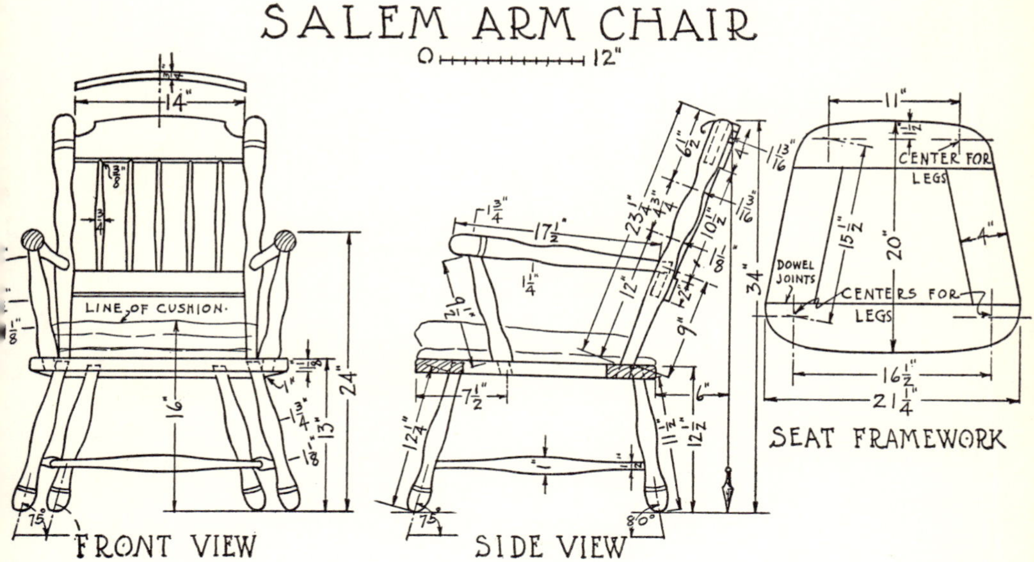

SALEM ARM CHAIR

0 ⊢—————⊣ 12"

FRONT VIEW

SIDE VIEW

SEAT FRAMEWORK

LINE OF CUSHION.

CENTER FOR LEGS

DOWEL JOINTS

CENTERS FOR LEGS

PLATE 72

SALEM ARM CHAIR

This chair is equally well suited for living room or bedroom. A splendid woodturning project, of sturdy construction, to be made out of maple or other hardwood and finished in an antique effect. Use foam rubber for upholstering the cushion. Plate 72, Fig. 113.

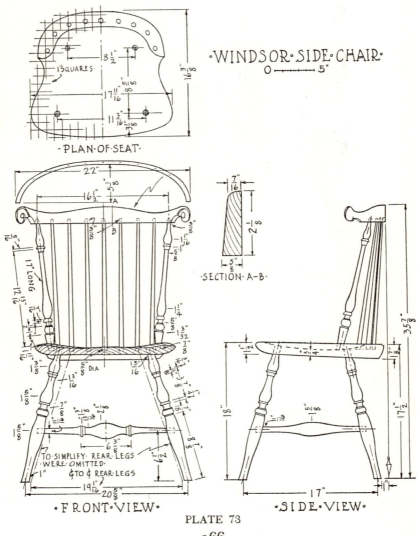

·PLAN·OF·SEAT·

·WINDSOR·SIDE·CHAIR·

·SECTION·A-B·

·FRONT·VIEW·

·SIDE·VIEW·

PLATE 73

166

FIGURE 119. American Windsor sidechair. An excellent project for the lathe. Use a steady-rest on all pieces.

WINDSOR SIDE CHAIR

A faithful reproduction of an old Colonial chair that I was permitted to copy. The legs, stretchers, and two back pieces are all simple spindle turning. The slender spindles of the back section must be turned by the aid of a steady-rest, Fig. 117. The seat should be made of two pieces glued together. The back rail is best made of hickory, steamed and bent in a form.

Use curly maple or other hardwood. Plate 73, Fig. 119.

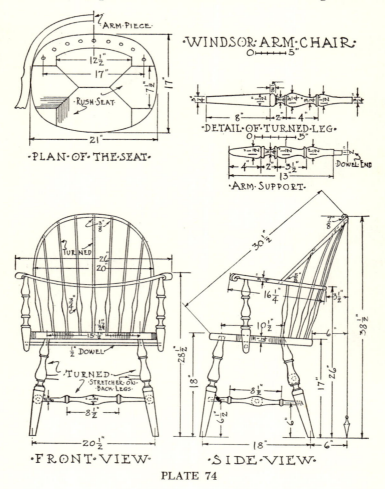

PLATE 74

WINDSOR ARMCHAIR

This armchair of old Colonial design is a good companion piece to the Windsor side chair, Fig. 119. The back and arm

168

FIGURE 120. Windsor armchair and butterfly table.
The chair can be made almost entirely on a lathe.

pieces must be steamed and bent in a form. For these pieces use hickory, since it bends quite easily. The seat frame is doweled together and then the rush bottom is woven.

Maple, birch, beech, or other hardwoods will be satisfactory to use. Plate 74, Fig. 120.

169

FIGURE 121. This small drum sander is very useful for cleaning up concave pieces.

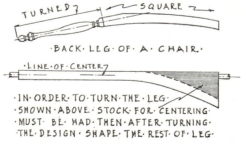

FIGURE 122

CRICKET BRIDGE LAMP

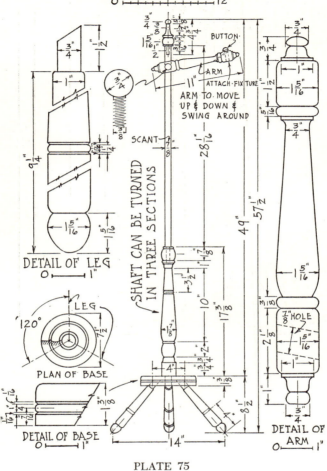

PLATE 75

CRICKET BRIDGE LAMP

This is a good woodturning project that has been simplified by making the shaft in three sections as shown. Use a hardwood such as maple, birch, beech, walnut, etc. Plate 75, Fig. 113.

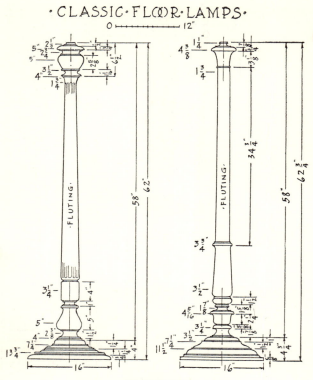

PLATE 76

Classic Floor Lamps

The shafts for these lamps must be turned with the aid of a steady-rest, Fig. 117. In order to get a hole through the shaft, make this of two pieces with a groove in each piece. Then glue together.

The base must be turned on the outside spindle of the lathe, using a large faceplate and pedestal tool rest. Fig. 2.

If this project is to be gilded, then use a close-grained soft-wood. Plate 76.

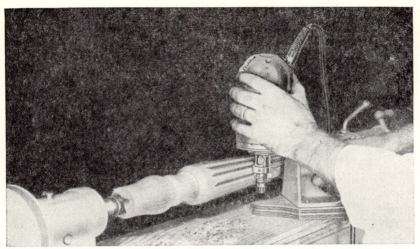

FIGURE 123. Reeding with a portable shaper. NOTE: Fluting can also be done in this manner.

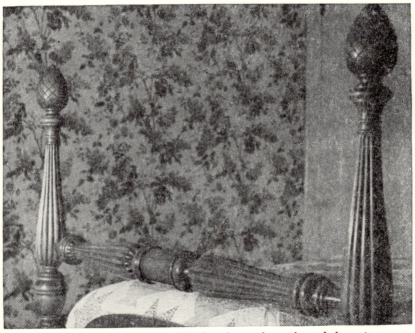

FIGURE 124. Bed posts made of curly maple, with reeded portions and carved pineapple tops.

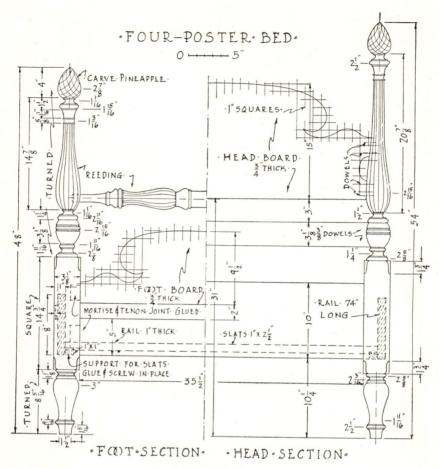

·FOUR–POSTER·BED·

0 ⊢———⊣ 5"

·CARVE·PINEAPPLE·

·I"SQUARES·

·HEAD·BOARD·
¾ THICK·

·TURNED·

·REEDING·

DOWELS

DOWELS

·FOOT·BOARD·
¾ THICK

MORTISE & TENON·JOINT·GLUED·

·RAIL·74"
LONG·

·RAIL·I"THICK·

·SLATS·I"x 2½·

·SUPPORT·FOR·SLATS·
GLUE & SCREW·IN·PLACE·

SQUARE

TURNED·

·FOOT·SECTION·   ·HEAD·SECTION·

PLATE 77

FOUR-POSTER BED

A fine Colonial design with medium height posts. A difficult
piece to make but beautiful when completed.

The posts are reeded, Fig. 123. The bed here pictured is
made of curly maple. Plate 77, Fig. 124.

FIGURE 125. Twin high four-poster beds. Use a steady-rest when turning
the posts and end spindle.

HIGH FOUR-POSTER BED

For those who like a bed with high posts, I recommend this
design. The posts and stretchers must be turned by the aid of a
steady-rest. Fig. 117.

These twin beds were made of mahogany. Plate 78, Fig.
125.

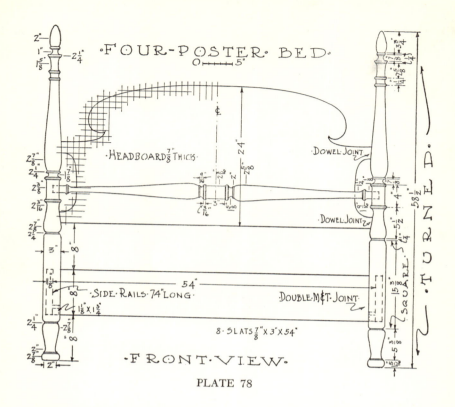

·FOUR-POSTER· BED·

·HEADBOARD ⅞" Thick·

·Dowel Joint·

·Dowel Joint·

·Side·Rails· 74" Long·

·Double·M&T·Joint·

8· SLATS ⅞"× 3"× 54"

·FRONT·VIEW·

PLATE 78

FIGURE 126. The four important steps are here shown for working out a spiral. Step 1. The laying out of the spiral by means of wrapping heavy paper around the cylinder and marking between the edges of the strip.

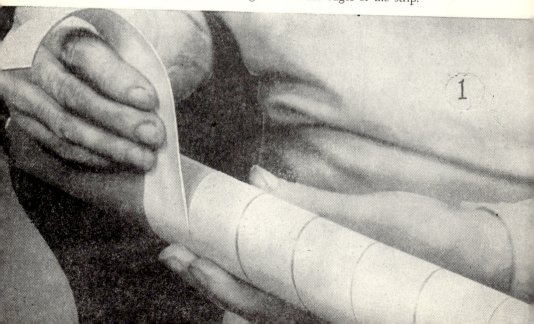

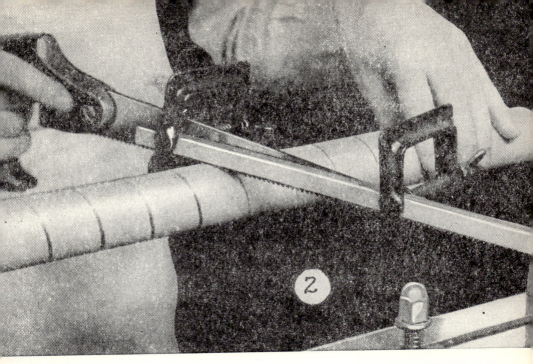

Step 2. Here saw accurately between the ridge lines as shown. A stop block is clamped to the saw to determine the depth of the cut.

Step 3 shows the wood rasp used to rough out the hollow of the spiral, the saw cut serving as a guide and depth indicator. After a uniform groove is formed, the edges are rounded over the ridge line.

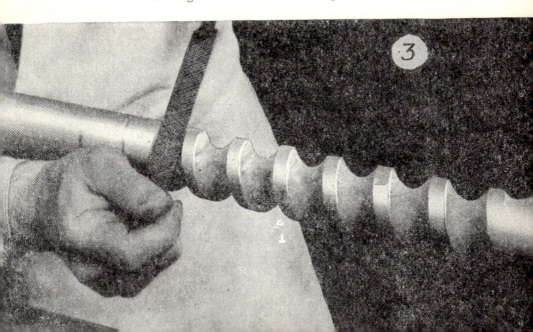

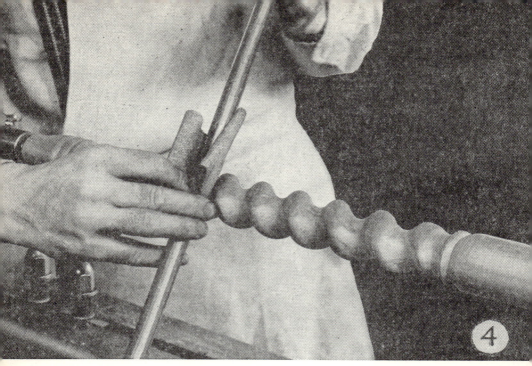

Step 4. Run the lathe at low speed and clean up the spiral with sandpaper, as shown.

INDEX

F

G

H

R

Racks, for towels, 64–65, 164
Rare woods, finishing, 53–54
Ring toss, 107–108
Rolling pin, 71–73
Rosettes, 87–89
Rosewood, for gavel, 70
Roughing stock, 26

S

Salad bowls, 97–100
Salem arm chair, 165–166
Sander, drum, 170
Sanding disk, 144
Sanding down, 50
Sandpaper, for Indian clubs, 58
Sandpapering, 51–52
Sandpapers, 46–47
Screw chuck, picture of, 77
Screwdriver handles, 61–63
Segment work, 135–138
Sewing set, 138–139
Sewing tray, 140–141
Shading with worn sandpaper, 50–51
Sharpening gouge and chisel, 18
Shellac, applying, 50–51
Ship's wheel mirror, 133–135
Shoulder, cutting of, 33–34
Silver gray finish, 53
Simplicity in design, 40–41
Sizer, 30
Skew chisel, smoothing with, 30–32
Smoker's outfit, 107–108
Smoking stand, 141
Smoothing with skew chisel, 30–32
Speed control, 13
Spindle feed handle, turning of, 24
Spiral turning, steps in, 176–178
Split turning, 77
Staining, 50
Steady-rest, 161
Stools, 109–111

T

U

V

W